HUMANITY

Other Books by Russell Genet

Real-Time Control with the TRS-80
Photoelectric Photometry of Variable Stars (with Douglas Hall)
Microcomputer Control of Telescopes (with Mark Trueblood)
Robotic Observatories (with Donald Hayes)
Telescope Control (with Mark Trueblood)

HUMANITY

THE CHIMPANZEES WHO WOULD BE ANTS

Russell Merle Genet

FOREWORD BY PETER J. RICHERSON

Collins Foundation Press

Humanity: The Chimpanzees Who Would Be Ants

Published by the Collins Foundation Press
4995 Santa Margarita Lake Road
Santa Margarita, CA 93453

Editor-in-Chief: Bette Carnrite
Cover design by John Davidson
Book design by Russell Genet
Ant and bonobo title page sketches by Cheryl Genet
Typography and composition by Cheryl Genet
Text set in Palatino Linotype, titles in Arial

Includes biographical references and an index

ISBN 0–9788441–0–6

Printed by Sheridan Books in the United States of America

Author's website: www.orionobservatory.org
Publisher's website: www.collinsff.org

DEDICATION

Cheryl Genet

My secret childhood sweetheart, who joined me and her brother Rich Fallick, my childhood pal, in our quest to find human meaning in a vast universe. After decades apart, she rejoined me as my wife to renew our cosmic quest in our golden years.

Dwight Collins

My buddy and confidant of three decades who not only helped me think through this book's predecessor while camping with me on the beaches of New Zealand and in the mountains of Arizona, but whose foundation kindly published this current volume.

Peter Richerson

My good friend and mentor in the modern theory of cultural evolution, which he co-developed with Robert Boyd.

David Poore

My seventh grade teacher and friend of five decades who, having whetted my intellectual appetite in class, shrewdly hinted that humanity's accumulated knowledge was patiently waiting for me at the well-stocked local public library.

CONTENTS

FOREWORD

In *Humanity,* Russ Genet pioneers a new genre of science writing. Modern science is on the horns of an intimidating dilemma. On one horn, science progresses by the labors of highly trained, highly specialized practitioners. Their resulting discoveries become ever more technical and difficult for others to appreciate except the discoverers' few fellow specialists. Russ himself is an astronomer, who in the past has specialized in the design of robotic telescopes, and who currently observes eclipsing binary stars, following the evolution of star spots and searching for orbiting planets. Wearing this hat, he is a typical specialist scientist.

On the other horn, we scientists inherently believe that all our understanding of the phenomena in the universe will, eventually, integrate into one whole. In principle, no scientific field can be isolated from any other. Any number of everyday scientific practices demonstrate the truth of this belief. For example, an archaeologist uses ^{14}Carbon and ^{40}Potassium radioisotope decay, electron spin resonance, and thermoluminescence as dating techniques. Archaeologists have to be part-time nuclear physicists to do their work. You never know what you might need to know.

Scientific research has increasingly become a team effort, since it takes several collaborating specialists to do cutting-edge work. I recently worked on a lake coring project. We produced two papers. One had seven authors, the other ten. My team reconstructed the last two hundred years or so of the lake's history by analyzing its layers of mud. These layers are deposited at the rate of a millimeter to a centimeter per year, and hold evidence of a rather large number of physical, chemical, and biological parameters of historical significance. Slice the core thin, take a few measurements, and you've got a history book. The more things you can measure, the better chance you have of reconstructing past events. Measuring and interpreting these various parameters takes specialized knowledge and equipment, so most measurements require a collaborator and a coauthor. It is not surprising that the average number of authors per scientific paper is rising inexorably across nearly all scientific disciplines.

Conventional training can only partially meet our need for ever-greater specialization, while helping us understand, to some degree, a broad and unpredictable swath of disciplines and sub-disciplines. My third-year biochemistry course used a slim textbook of perhaps 200 pages. Forty years later, my daughter's thick, first-year biology text included far more biochemistry than science had even known four decades before. Colleges demand more of today's students than they ever demanded of me. Perhaps as a result of more rigorous pedagogy, average IQs are rising at the rate of about 5 points per generation. Yet scientific knowledge is nearly doubling every generation, so the gap between what scientists need to know and what they can hope to learn is widening as surely as the number of authors per paper is rising. Furthermore, the rapid pace of discovery means that even the best training is quickly outmoded.

My colleague Rob Boyd pointed out to me some years ago how dependent scientists have become upon "popular" science books for their interdisciplinary education. These books are intended for the intelligent layperson. But, of course, scientists themselves are just intelligent laypersons as regards all disciplines and sub-disciplines except the few in which they have serious training. As one's knowledge in a particular area becomes dated, popular science is often the only practical method of keeping up with the times. If one wants to keep up across a broad front, popular science books and articles become, perforce, one's principal antennae.

The trouble is that the editorial standards for popular science are rather low. Many of its authors are journalists, not scientists. Their books lack the finger-tip feel that scientists have for their pet subjects. Even some of the very best of these books are lacking on the science side. Although some popular science writers are scientists, they often turn to this genre because they have an ax to grind.

Although Russ wrote this book as a scientist, it's primarily about subjects in which he does not specialize. Wearing the hat of a generalist, he had to depend substantially on secondary sources by journalists and (potentially) ax-grinding scientists. Since we all have views of our own, *perfection* in this regard is an unrealistic goal. Nevertheless, Russ aspired to raise the bar, and in this I believe he has succeeded brilliantly. By reading extensively and applying the scientist's ever-skeptical approach, he has synthesized the scientific story of humanity with remarkable fidelity to the central tendency of our current best account.

Russ would be the last to recommend that anyone read his book uncritically. However well he represents the current central tendency, he cannot do full justice to the variation in views among scientists, nor to all the details. Nor can he avoid the inevitable fact that the knowledge he conveys will be rapidly outmoded. Certainly, if you have a serious need to know about a particular area, you'll have to dig deeper. His "Further Reading" at the end of this book gives you a reliable start. Nevertheless, as a broad-spectrum antenna, this is the book to beat.

The alternate futures section of the book is perhaps where Russ's even-handed account is easiest to appreciate. Although every thinking person understands how hard the future is to predict, we fall all too easily into combining science with our personal preferences to concoct utopias and dystopias, investing them with a bogus degree of certitude. As Russ stresses, the four scenarios he develops by no means exhaust the possibilities, but they do serve effectively to make the two critical points. First, evolution can't be an exact predictive science. The range of possible futures is, if measurable at all, vast on an all-the-stars-in-the-galaxy scale. Second, we humans *potentially* have some real control over our fate. Writers typically pose a false dichotomy in this regard, suggesting that either we do control our fate or we don't.

The truth is much more interesting. We have some tools that can give us control over our future, and we can use these tools locally to good effect. As I wrote these words, I experienced one of California's common moderate, 6.5-magnitude earthquakes. In unprepared territory, such an earthquake can cause thousands of fatalities. California isn't perfectly prepared for a 6.5, but in this case, only two people died—in the collapse of an unreinforced masonry building deliberately left standing because of its historical significance. In principle, we can apply planning tools to reduce the threat of earthquakes, global climate change, and any other natural or man-made threats except the ultimate heat death of the universe. To do so, we need, as Russ puts it, to take on the major project of creating a new level of biological organization, a global superorganism.

The evidence of the last ten thousand years tells us that humans are adept at scaling up social organization to meet new threats and opportunities. We still have a lot to accomplish in a hurry, even on the comparatively rapid time scale of cultural evolution, so we have to bear down earnestly on this chore if we want to escape a bust scenario of one kind or another. It looks doable, but only if enough right-minded folk take their turn at the crank.

I hope you enjoy this book as much as I have.

Peter J. Richerson
University of California, Davis

PUBLISHER'S NOTE

I met Russell Genet more than 30 years ago in the US Air Force where we conducted joint research in the field of life-cycle cost analysis. We shared a belief that each of us had the opportunity to make the world a better place, and that science was one vehicle we could use to make our contribution. Russ's achievements since then, including the authorship of this book, demonstrate that this credo has served him well.

Russ loves science. He combines infectious excitement about his passion for research with exceptional analytic skills. He has an uncommon talent for rapidly assimilating the essence of an entire specialty through independent study and informal interaction with experts and then making important contributions to the field. He's done this at least four times: in the fields of rocket guidance systems, in life-cycle cost analysis, in the development of robotic telescopes—where he gained worldwide prominence—and, most recently, in integrating the overlapping fields addressed in this book.

Russ has demonstrated how much there is to gain by carefully synthesizing across scientific disciplines. The physical and social sciences sometimes offer conflicting explanations and insights as to how the human species evolved and where it is headed. On the one hand, specialization has been a key enabler for the flood of new knowledge that began with the fifteenth-century Renaissance. On the other hand, the current culture of scientific inquiry seldom condones the practice of looking across disciplinary boundaries to uncover insights that different fields of inquiry offer when considered together. Characteristically, Russ has refused to conform to this tradition. Indeed, the pages of this book took form from Russ's lifelong expedition through many fields. He has fine-tuned this process to an art.

Over the past decade, I have reviewed and offered editorial comment on much of the source material for *Humanity*. Serving in this role, I have relearned and vastly expanded my knowledge of humanity's history on our planet. It has provided me with an invaluable framework on which to weave together the threads of knowledge I have acquired over a lifetime—threads that include studies of our planet's evolution, geology, and ecology, as well as the history of human civilization, the world's religions, economics, psychology, and sociology.

My editorial activities have changed my understanding of humanity. I have a new context in which to view our human experience and our planet's history. I have a new respect and reverence for the exquisite interdependence between the human species and the millions of other life forms with which we share the finite resources of planet Earth. I now see my fellow humans and myself as participants in a web of life that has maintained its balance for millions of years before we even arrived. Nature—with which I've always felt kinship from early explorations in the woods and mountains surrounding my childhood home—appears more beautiful and mystifying than ever. I now invest more of my time considering how to care for and nurture life around me.

My work with Russ has also influenced my opinions about how we conduct ourselves in our planetary home. Humanity's focus on its internal politics and rivalries seems almost trivial, relative to the challenges we face as a species in bringing about harmony with our natural environment and sustainability on the planet. These thoughts humble me and give me more compassion for the people I know and for the millions I do not. I am grateful to Russ for the role he has played in my acquisition of these rich perspectives.

Dwight Collins, President
Collins Family Foundation

ACKNOWLEDGEMENTS
A Team Effort

My thanks to my close friend and colleague of many decades, Dwight Collins, for encouraging and supporting me in my science-based grand synthesis. Thanks also to my good friend and mentor Peter Richerson. Pete independently drew the same conclusion about humanity that I have have drawn: that we are, in our most basic essence, superorganisms similar to ant colonies.

My thanks to Bette Carnrite for her meticulous work as Editor-in-Chief and to Cheryl Genet, David Genet, Elissa Hansen, Kenneth Kissell, Dannielle Tassell, Richard Trowbridge, and Vera Wallen who read the entire manuscript, cover-to-cover, suggesting hundreds of improvements. I deeply appreciate others who contributed their time and talents as well, among them Connie Barlow, Lorraine Donegan, Michael Dowd, Kristina Downer, and Janice Go.

Finally, I acknowledge the support of my wife Cheryl. We began the quest to understand humanity some fifty-four years ago, spending many happy hours together with her brother Rich addressing the big questions. Their home, the Rainbow Ranch, was just a short distance from my own ranch; both were nestled in a peaceful and remote valley in the San Bernardino Mountains of Southern California.

When I was seventeen we parted ways, not to see each other again for almost four decades. But in the end, I found her again, courted her, and we were married. Although the coyotes no longer howl at night at the original Rainbow Ranch—it was subdivided long ago—we found a new remote, peaceful little valley on California's central coast. At Santa Margarita Lake, near San Luis Obispo, the coyotes still howl and the deer still graze in our yard. We named our new home Rainbow's End. Surrounded by our beloved books, together we continue our quest for human meaning in a vast universe.

PREFACE
Science, synthesis, and story

The story you are about to read is science's story of the cosmos and humanity, or, more precisely, one version of science's current story. Although science usually does not concern itself with grand syntheses across what, in reality, are a number of separate sciences, each with its own point of view, a few scientists, such as myself, cannot resist attempting to pull all the pieces together. To accomplish this, I borrowed all the pieces from experts in their fields, assembling them into a coherent story.

Borrowing ideas isn't easy, however. I didn't have the inclination to take dozens of university courses in biology, the social sciences, and history. Nor was I patient enough to wade through a stack of strangely worded, expensive textbooks, each loaded down with tons of unwanted trivia. So I borrowed the science for my story from low-cost, easy-to-read science "trade" books. Written by eminent scientists for the edification of the unwashed masses, they were relatively easy pickings. These volumes are all dog-eared now, full of notes scribbled in their margins. I am deeply indebted to these literate scientists. Their wonderful books are listed at the end of this book under "Further Reading." I highly recommend them all.

Finally, let me mention my comrades-in-arms; other grand synthesizers who, like me, could not resist presenting, in easily-read book form, science's comprehensive evolutionary picture of what came before humanity, how we came to be and, for some authors, where we might be headed. Listed for your reading pleasure under "Preface" in "Further Reading" at the end of this book are my favorites. Each has its own slant, its own take, but in the final analysis, they all tell the same story. I hope you will continue to explore science's story of how we came to be.

PROLOGUE
In a nutshell

The evolutionary epic is probably
the best myth we will ever have.
Edward O. Wilson

The evolution of the human species is
one of the greatest dramas in the unfolding of life on Earth—
a tale of passion, challenge, and high adventure,
with everyone's favorite character, themselves, *in the lead role.*
William F. Allman

The program that is given out before plays and operas—especially for performances in a language foreign to the audience—often provides a synopsis, a story in a nutshell, of what is about to be presented. Given below in this prologue, is such a synopsis, the story of humanity in a nutshell.

Our story doesn't start with humanity itself, however. Before we can raise the curtain, we must sprinkle our cosmic stage with stars for energy and planets for life. And we will need to throw the switch labeled "life" to "on," allowing life to evolve over the eons into diverse creatures. The first two chapters, *Cosmos* and *Life*, are these astronomical and biological "stage setters."

The curtain finally raises on *Ants*, our human civilizational analogues, and soon *Chimpanzees*, our closest genetic relatives enter, stage left. The story then continues with *Hominids*, the tale of how our ancestors bravely the faced lions and other dangers in an increasingly treeless east African savanna, while our two sister species, the common chimpanzees and the bonobos, stayed behind in their protective western jungle. They never left their Garden of Eden, while we hominids ventured forth to become the planet's top hunter-gatherers. Although not numerous—eating steak at the top of the food chain limits one's numbers—by the end of the last ice age we dwelt in every continent except Antarctica. Finally, at the very end of this act, *Homo sapiens* enter, stage right.

We are the only surviving species in the hominid line and we became numerous instead of rare by taking up agriculture. Ants, long before us, had become numerous in the same way. They developed ingenious herding and gardening skills that allowed them to tap the plentiful food at the bottom of the food chain. We simply aped the ants. By feeding off the bottom of the food chain instead of the top—eating beans instead of steak—our population soared, and soon the number of individuals in each human civilization, like each ant colony, could be counted in the thousands or millions.

There was, however, a fly in the evolutionary ointment. Other life had thoughtfully restrained the ants' success, but we were not so fortunate. Evolving our simple chimp tools into machines, we tapped a bonanza of food and fossil fuel energy. We were an irresistible team, we humans and our domesticated plants and animals—not to mention our chain saws, bulldozers, and tractors. We quickly blitzkrieged the planet; no other life could stop us as we rushed headlong towards the sustainable limits of the planet.

So what is our fate? How will our story end? Four alternative story endings are offered; take your pick. Reversing direction, will we return to a planetary Garden of Eden, rejoining our sister chimpanzees in harmony with other life? Or, pedal to the metal, will we slam full speed into the wall of planetary finiteness, crashing into oblivion? Then again, with only modest restraint will we transform the entire earth into one gigantic yet sustainable global farm? But why limit ourselves to earth? Why not leave our birth-planet behind, voyage to the stars with our machine partners and, with some future Captain Kirk at the helm, establish a galactic empire and explore the magnificent universe that gave us birth?

PART I

What Came Before Humanity?
Setting the Stage

The universe is an evolving product of an evolutionary process.
It is not an accident; it is an enterprise.
Theodosius Dobzhansky

Despite all the stars and galaxies that form a backdrop,
cosmic evolution is a story that places
life and humanity on center stage—
and that's not an anthropocentric statement
as much as an honest statement about
human curiosity and inventiveness.
Eric Chaisson

Chapter 1

COSMOS
Stars and planets for life

Had I been present at the Creation, I would have given some useful hints for the better ordering of the universe.

Alfonse the Wise

Given the appropriate context of specific laws and physical conditions, chance becomes creative.

Hubert Reeves

In the beginning ...

Once upon a time there was a Big Bang. The scientists who study the entire universe—the cosmologists—generally prefer not to speculate about the cause of the Big Bang, although some have been heard to mumble a few words about "fluctuations in the cosmic void" and the like. However, when considering the state of the universe when it was just a trillionth of a trillionth of a second old, they feel they are on solid ground and reasonably confident in their scientific description.

So our story, being a scientific tale, should actually start with, "Almost in the beginning there was a Big Bang, and very near the beginning, the simplest, lowest-level modules—the quarks—came into existence. These quarks occasionally came together to form the next-highest level, atomic particles, only to be instantly torn apart again in the hectic agitation caused by the immense heat. If, in some giant cosmic experiment, we could have arranged for the universe to immediately stop its expansion and cooling, it would have remained a hot, simple sea of quarks. Higher-level modules would have been too fragile to exist at this elevated temperature. Thankfully, however, this didn't happen. The universe continued expanding and quarks combined to form the next level in the hierarchy—a virtual zoo of different subatomic particles. The most stable—and hence most common of these—were familiar particles such as protons and neutrons. At this point, we can already discern a simple evolutionary process at work in the universe. Lower-level modules randomly come together to form higher-level modules, most of which quickly fall apart, while a few sturdier, more stable modules hang together. Over time, the stable assemblies accumulate at the expense of the less stable; the latter are constantly knocked apart and reassembled until they finally hit on a stable combination. Recycling, it seems, has a long history. This selection for stability was a directional process that caused the universe to evolve from simpler to more complex entities as its temperature fell. We call this affinity for stability "physical selection" to distinguish it from other types of evolutionary selection which we will encounter at higher levels of complexity.

Primordial nucleosynthesis—the porridge gets too cold

As the universe expanded and cooled, subatomic particles formed atomic nuclei, the central cores of atoms, building up from hydrogen, the simplest, to helium, only slightly more complex. By the time the universe was only three minutes old, it had become too cold for the building process beyond helium to continue, so construction of the hierarchy of complexity stopped dead in its tracks. While too high a temperature tears higher-level modules apart as quickly as they form, too cold a temperature freezes lower-level modules into inactivity, since insufficient energy is available to form any higher-level modules. Chaotic hyperactivity to frozen inactivity in only three minutes—that's our universe!

From the above, we infer one of the general laws of the universe, the Goldilocks Principle: to build any given level in the hierarchy of complexity, there are temperatures that are too hot, temperatures that are too cold, and a temperature that is just right. As complexity increases, the "just-right" temperature decreases. We might have expected this: the more complex the assemblage, the more delicate, and thus more easily it is disrupted by heat. Another way of viewing this concept is that growth in complexity occurs at the boundary between disorganized chaos and rigid order, between hot hyperactivity and frozen inaction.

At this point in cosmic history, we can also discern a second general law of the universe: even given the proper temperature, it takes time to create higher levels of complexity, time for the lower-level modules to combine in various ways, to search for and accumulate the most stable combinations. Our universe cooled so fast that atomic nuclei more complex than hydrogen and helium simply didn't have time to form. The "porridge" had gotten too cold. It isn't entirely clear why the universe was in such a hell-fire rush.

It is a good thing the universe cooled rapidly, however, for had it cooled more slowly, matter would soon have evolved to its most stable state—iron—and that, for sure, would have been the end of our story. By cooling rapidly—supercooling—the hydrogen and helium had the potential for further evolution, for providing the fuel that could allow the universe to keep on ticking for eons.

Stellar furnaces—some like it hot

Gravity slowly but inexorably gathered hydrogen and helium atoms into galaxies and knitted these, in turn, into the ever–more–concentrated matter we call stars. Stars bucked the general cosmic trend of expansion and cooling, albeit just in small, localized areas. Stars reheated the porridge, as it were. When a star's temperature got "just right," the buildup of complexity continued, as heavier elements beyond helium were forged into ever–heavier elements and stars released hot, high–energy photons into an increasingly cold universe. This flow of energetic photons into cold space would, later on, be crucial to life.

But there was another show-stopping difficulty here; it lay in the process of forming more complex atomic nuclei in the centers of stars by unceremoniously slamming simpler nuclei together. There was, sadly, no stable combination of helium that could form carbon. Though these elements could assemble, they flew apart again in a mere trillionth of a second. From this process we get a hint of a possible third general law: if all higher-level combinations are unstable, hierarchical growth will stop, leaving only simpler groupings. Fortunately, however, that fleeting trillionth of a second provided the escape from this third law that allowed the universe to continue along its path to greater complexity. In the brief instant two helium nuclei came together, a third helium nucleus would, once in a great while, bang into and join them. From this unlikely process, highly stable carbon was formed. It was so stable that the process was irreversible, a one-way nuclear-evolutionary ratchet. Slowly (over billions of years for typical stars), a never-ending trickle of helium nuclei triplets found their way past the instability barrier to the stable, higher-complexity haven of carbon.

This process gives us a clue to yet another universal law: it isn't the highly probable, easy, lower-level combinations that matters; it's the stability of the less probable, more difficult combinations that count in the long run. The universe's patience is unrivaled. It can wait as long as necessary for progress to occur.

Once nuclei in the hot centers of the more massive stars passed through the bottleneck to stable carbon, they continued their buildup of ever-increasing atomic complexity until they reached iron. Iron is the most stable of all atomic elements. The heavier nuclei beyond iron absorb energy as they form, instead of releasing energy during their genesis. When a star converts the last of its hot center into iron, its supply of nuclear energy is exhausted; its furnace is extinguished. Without the outward pressure from the nuclear fire, the star instantly collapses, often rebounding in a spectacular supernova explosion. For a glorious few hours or days, a supernova star outshines an entire galaxy of billions of suns. In the process, it creates the less stable atomic nuclei beyond iron, pumping gravitational energy from the collapse and subsequent explosion into their creation. In this way, the last half of the ninety-two natural elements were created. The atomic level on the ladder of complexity was finally completed, within stars, long after the hierarchy began with the formation of hydrogen and helium during the first three minutes of the universe.

Molecules create complexity

Moving beyond the hot interior of stars, once matter became cool enough for atomic nuclei to capture electrons and thus become proper atoms, such atoms could combine with each other electrically to form the multi-atom assemblies we call molecules. Such atomic combinations were the next level in the hierarchy of complexity. It was cool enough in the outer atmosphere of the coolest stars for a number of relatively simple molecules to form, although too hot for truly complex molecules to assemble themselves. In the cold of space not far from stars, simple molecules could also materialize, though here it was too cold for complex molecules to form. Advances in molecular complexity required a temperature cooler than that of the stars, yet warmer than the frigidity of space. Not too hot, not too cold—picky Goldilocks required properly situated planets with temperature–stabilizing atmospheres to support complex molecules and thereby continue the evolution of complexity.

Scientists can duplicate the physical conditions between the hot atmospheres of stars and the cold of nearby space. By allowing a variety of atoms and simple molecules to react under wide-ranging physical conditions, they have determined which combinations can lead to the formation of complex molecules. The three required conditions which favor the buildup of complex molecules are: (1) temperatures and pressures such that the common molecule, H_2O, exists in a liquid state (water); (2) a gentle flow of energy that keeps the ingredients stirred up; and (3) a steady supply of common elements, including carbon. Carbon, with its symmetrical four-hook arrangement, easily binds with itself to form the backbones of most naturally occurring complex molecules.

Hydrogen and helium, formed in the universe's first three minutes, remain its two most common elements, comprising over 99% of cosmic matter. The other 1%, matter generated within stars and occasionally flung out into space, remains in its elementary atomic form or in simple chemical compounds in the coolest stars or warmest space. Only a minuscule amount of matter exists under the three key conditions (water, gentle energy flow, and a ready supply of vital elements such as carbon) to achieve any further growth in complexity. As far as we know, these conditions exist naturally only on or near the surfaces of planets. Knowing this, we can infer another general law of the universe: as complexity increases, the portion of the universe involved in such complexification rapidly diminishes.

Catch-22 – The end of the line?

There appear to be limits, however, to the natural growth of physical complexity. Under the most ideal planetary conditions, with the best possible selection of elements and an optimal amount of energy flowing from a planet's star, a point comes in the growth of complexity where the filigreed carbon-chain structures break up as fast as random chance brings them together. Although single carbon atoms themselves are very stable molecules, chains of carbon atoms linked together are not nearly as stable. In fact, molecules in general are less stable than atoms and, unlike the sturdy elementary particles, atoms, and simple molecules, complex molecules are relatively flimsy.

Furthermore, the most complex molecules are the most delicate, lacking much inherent stability. They easily fall apart soon after they are assembled. Rare, highly complex molecules simply didn't hang around long after being formed. They didn't persist long enough to form the basis of an even higher level of complexity. The universe had painted itself into a complexity-instability corner. It was a Catch-22: if molecules were more complex, they couldn't be stable; if they were stable, they couldn't be more complex.

So there we have it: the evolutionary progression of complexity from the Big Bang to complex molecules summarized as four hierarchical levels—quarks, subatomic particles, atoms, and molecules—from the simplest to the most complex. For almost the entire universe, this is the total and complete story, the story of physical evolution—the end, *fini,* close the book. We astronomers and our good friends, the nuclear physicists, think it is a great story. Our story covers almost all of the matter in the universe and includes all the stars, galaxies, and dust, etc. However, just for you my dear readers, who are made of highly complex assemblages of atoms formed from the miniscule remainder, I will continue on with science's story and how evolution overcame the "Catch-22" of molecular complexity.

Chapter 2

LIFE
Nature's road to complexity

What evolution does is to give the arrow of time a barb,
which stops it from running backward,
and once it has this barb, the chance play of errors
will take it forward of itself.
Jacob Bronowski

The gravity of entropy cannot be defied;
but as the crest forever falls,
biological order rides it down like a surfer.
Kevin Kelly

Going round in circles—autocatalytic cycles

As described in Chapter 1, *Cosmos,* the universe had painted itself into a complexity-instability corner. Logically, the only way out of this corner was for the universe to compensate for the inherent instability of complex molecules by creating them more frequently than random chance allowed. On planet Earth, nature did exactly that. It produced large numbers of uniform, complex molecules faster than they could decay. Give nature an inch of wiggle room, and she will make a mile of complexification.

Fortunately for us, and all other life, the chemistry of the universe is such that one molecule can act as a tool to build another, becoming a catalyst that attracts and holds the appropriate atoms in place until they have time to snap together. Under normal conditions, atoms rarely come together to create a complex molecule, but with appropriate electrostatic enticements through the guidance of catalyst molecular tools, the formation of complex molecules can become highly probable. We come now to the key turning point in our story of the evolution of complexity. Using its patient, trial and error method, nature discovered that these molecular tools could make other tools.

Finding the chemical secret of life itself, evolution eventually placed molecular tools in a ring: tool A made tool B, tool B made tool C, and tool C made tool A. Such a ring, called an autocatalytic cycle, could spew out copious quantities of identical complex molecules, as long as the raw ingredients and energy consumed in the process continued to be available. This autocatalytic cycle breached the barrier of inherent instability by generating large amounts of complex molecules. Who cared if they decayed? Their instability was of little consequence as long as the autocatalytic process churned them out faster than they could fall apart, as long as there were enough of them to form the basis for the next higher level in the hierarchy of complexity.

By the way, the most famously spectacular of autocatalytic cycles is the BZ chemical reaction. It was named after Boris Belousov, who discovered it, and Anatoly Zhabotinskii, who convinced incredulous chemists it was a reality. Confined to a thin layer in a glass dish, the BZ reaction produces dramatically spiraling waves of bright colors that show observable structures forming from a chemical stew.

There were two inherent difficulties, however, with the autocatalytic path to increased complexity. First, it had to be initialized by a somewhat improbable combination of several complex tools that made each other in a closed cycle. Second, once this cycle got started it had to keep going continuously. If there were any interruptions anywhere in the cycle for any reason whatsoever (such as a lack of one of the raw materials), the tools, now no longer being freshly produced, would soon decay, and the vital information—the randomly discovered magical combination that made it all work—would be lost.

Nature found a randomly generated setup of several complex molecules involved in a self-perpetuating, tool-builds-tool cycle in less than a hundred million years—a mere blink of the cosmic evolutionary eye. Then nature solved the second difficulty—that of avoiding a killer gap in the cycle of one chemical producing another—in an incredibly clever manner.

Occasional tool-making errors in the cycle were unavoidable. Even with catalysts, molecules don't always click into place correctly. Most errors were naturally and instantly self-limiting and usually fatal. On rare occasions, however, such glitches persisted without breaking the cycle. In those cases, two slightly different cycles existed, each running alongside the other: the original cycle without the error and the new one with the error. Similar "mistakes" eventually occurred in these two descendant lines. Most of them perished, but a few survived and multiplied. Thus, the original parent cycle proliferated into an ever expanding number of daughter cycles. Those chemical cycles with the best "information" grabbed the most resources, reproduced the fastest, and became the most numerous. The rules of success were, in short, have the right information to allow one to consume voraciously, copy quickly and (mostly) accurately, and, never, ever, pause or even slow down.

Now, here's the clever part of nature's selection. Those lines of descent that, for any reason whatsoever, developed a gap in their cycle (such as a tool that wasn't made) were instantly eliminated forever. One strike, you're out—no second, let alone third strike, in this game! Thus, surviving lines, by definition, had never failed to consume and reproduce in their entire history, a history now 3.8 billion years old. As a result, surviving lines on our planet never lost the magic combination of the first cycle, although as change piled on change, the original tool-makes-tool sequences were greatly altered and expanded in daughter lines. As various daughter lines competed against each other, the original information proliferated into many different lines of descent. These lines accumulated "survival information" over time as the less-informed, less-efficient lines were squeezed out by their environmentally better-adapted sisters. Thus it was that the descendants of what began as a cyclic chemical process continued, at least on this planet, in the uninterrupted process we call life. Life added new levels of complexity to a hierarchy that stretched back to the Big Bang itself.

Cells—keeping it all together

Soon (perhaps even at the beginning), evolution produced a number of autocatalytic chemical cycles enclosed in a container, the cell, that kept the reactants from drifting away and breaking the cycle. Life had begun. Unlike the BZ autocatalytic reaction, which has to be started and maintained by chemists concentrating appropriate reactants in a glass container, life maintains information on what reactants it needs and, critically, on how to obtain them. Life even provides its own "glass containers"—cells. Also, in contrast to the BZ reaction, which obediently stays in its original dish, life endlessly multiplies its containers until it runs out of resources, chokes to death on its own degraded waste products, encounters limits imposed on it by other life, or covers the entire planet. Every life-form is a would-be planetary king.

Life is about metabolism. It maintains itself by capturing high-grade energy and nutrients, thus avoiding the remorseless decay imposed by the Second Law of Thermodynamics. Life is an unbroken chain of information, accumulated over the generations. Life has learned how to use the Second Law to its own advantage and create ever more of itself in competition (or sometimes in cooperation) with other lines of life, all trying to be the best at playing the same game. The second law may win in the end, trillions of years from now; however, current life doesn't seem to be too concerned about this eventuality.

The story of life on Earth is the story of how various lines of descent accumulated survival information over time—how some lines continued relatively unchanged at lower levels of complexity, while others evolved to ever-higher levels in (surprise) a hierarchical manner. Simpler living "modules" combined cooperatively to form higher-level modules. These higher-level modules, in turn, eventually provided the basis for even loftier levels of complexity.

Movements between life's hierarchical levels were *The Major Transitions in Evolution,* as captured in the title of a pioneering book by John Maynard Smith and Eors Szathmáry. They suggest that at each level in the hierarchy of life, structural limitations on the amount of information that life could accumulate to refine its techniques for eating and reproducing in an increasingly competitive world, eventually brought the growth of complexity to a halt. Each major transition took place when life devised some new method for accumulating, storing, or reproducing information that overcame previous limitations. Life made most of these transitions by combining or merging lower-level modules together into a cooperative "team," thus continuing, in a way, the tradition established before life by quarks, particles, atoms, and molecules. Let's now work our way up life's hierarchy of complexity, overcoming one information roadblock at a time.

DNA—life's how–to–assemble–it manual

It has been suggested that as the number of different chemical tools within the early cells grew to the hundreds and eventually even thousands, and the individual tools became larger and more complex, the total number of any specific tool type within a given cell necessarily decreased—not enough room at the inn. The number and the complexity of different tool types were eventually limited by the random process that split the tools into two independent, yet hopefully complete, tool kits during cell division. If one tool type out of hundreds or even thousands was missing, just one, the daughter cell with the missing tool would die, its intricate and intermeshed chemical cycles grinding to a halt.

The obvious solution to this roadblock to the growth of complexity was to somehow make certain that when the cell split in two, at least one tool of each type was somehow placed in each of the two daughter cells' tool kits. Evolution accomplished this trick with its usual masterful ingenuity. It separated the information on the production of chemical tools from the tools themselves. Thus, when a cell split, the cell duplicated the information on how to make the tools a single time and gave one complete set of information to each daughter cell. In other words, instead of splitting up the self-replicating tools, life made two copies of a "manual" that explained how to assemble these tools.

This chemical tool assembly information was encoded as four letters, twenty-two words (each word always consisted of exactly three letters, denoting a tool sub-part), and multiple-word paragraphs (each specifying how to assemble an entire tool). Together, these paragraphs (genes), typically ten thousand or more, constituted a small book instructing cells how and in what order to assemble all the different chemical tools they needed to survive. The "manual" was, of course, the famous DNA molecule. A cell read the encoded information, translated it into a useful form, and proceeded to make the tools. The tools then set about their normal chemical cyclic thing: eating raw materials, excreting wastes, and producing more of themselves until the cell grew big, fat, and ready to divide.

As computer buffs will recognize, the very act of reading encoded information itself requires a modicum of un-encoded information, the so-called "boot-up" instructions. When a cell divides, it must contain enough copies of old-fashioned, un-encoded instructions so that at least one complete boot-up guide makes it to each daughter cell. Among most animals, this boot-up information is passed along the female line. That means females pass more information to future generations than males do. (Some things in life never change.)

With life's information getting copied just once during reproduction, and with each daughter cell needing only a single copy, the amount of information a cell could physically contain and pass on was orders of magnitude greater than that of cells prior to such encoding. With this new, greatly expanded capability for handling information, bacteria (i.e. prokaryotes), the first to test drive this hot new model, had a complexity-building field day for a couple of billion years.

Bacteria invented photosynthesis, making sunlight energy directly available to life. This resulted, ironically, in a massive poisoning of the atmosphere with waste oxygen. Some very clever bacteria soon figured out how to use the poisonous oxygen to extract even greater energy from food. One critter's trash is another critter's treasure. Bacteria went on, as John Postgate describes in *The Outer Reaches of Life*, to work out all the difficult and exotic chemical pathways that exploited the various niches for life on this planet. Human biochemists still lag far behind the genetically clever bacteria. By a billion years ago, these biochemical whiz-kids had successfully discovered most of the really nifty chemical reactions. Bacteria were the great inventors. Hierarchical levels that later followed these innovators were, to use a tasty metaphor, mere frosting on the microbial cake.

Parallel Xerox machines and library stacks

After a couple of billion years of brilliant accomplishments by bacterial life, the amount of information that a single, modest-sized DNA book could accumulate—considerable as it was—finally became the limiting factor in the further accrual of information. It's not that the prokaryote cells didn't have room for bigger books; DNA books are, after all, very compact. The problem was that bigger books take more time to copy, and cells that took too long to reproduce died out. In times of plenty, those that copied quickly out-reproduced their slower counterparts, eventually replacing them. The DNA copy process starts at one point on the DNA "necklace" and works its way around in both directions to the opposite end. This process can move along the necklace only so fast. As books of DNA instructions on how the cell could assemble all the chemical tools needed for survival got larger, they eventually reached a point at which the disadvantage of slowness in reproduction offset the advantage of any additional information. The growth of complexity had stalled out again.

Life's solution, this time, was one that anyone familiar with libraries and copy machines will instantly recognize: break the single book of information up into a number of separate, much smaller books. Arrange these smaller books in an orderly manner on shelves in a central library and have multiple Xerox machines standing by, one for each book. When the race to reproduce begins, simultaneously take all the books off the shelves, copy them in parallel on the multiple copy machines (one per book), and then put the books back on the shelves. No matter how large the library, the copy time is just that of one small book, a clear illustration of the power of parallelism in action. This new, multi-book-library type of life is easy to distinguish from the single-book bacteria that preceded it, as its information is arranged in orderly chromosome stacks in a central nucleus library. These library (nucleated) cells are the eukaryotes. Earlier single-book bacteria are the prokaryotes. Biologist Lynn Margulis made a convincing case that it was the merging of different lower-level prokaryotes that formed the higher-level eukaryotes.

Multicellularity—billions of identical libraries

With an entire library of books at their disposal, cells were no longer limited by the amount of information they could access. Life evolved, becoming ever more complex, until it pushed cells to the point where their basic physical limitations finally restrained further increases in size and complexity. Cells took in nutrients and excreted wastes through their outer surfaces, their cellular walls. As they evolved to ever-larger sizes, their volumes increased much more rapidly than their surface areas. Cells eventually reached a size at which their surface area couldn't support any further increase in volume. This volume for most cells was small and had to remain so.

Furthermore, any one type of cell could do only so much. The various types of cells were separate, competing lines of descent, independently reproducing and attending to their own business. Cooperation was, generally, missing among different types of specialized cells. Such cooperation could take place only if cells were not competitive—that is if they descended from the same line (and thus genetically mirrored each other and shared the same reproduction). Ever the inventive MacGyver, life employed the excess informational storage capabilities inherent in central library cells to solve this problem. The solution was to have specialized cells use different portions of identical copies of the same library. In this way, each cell, regardless of its type, contained the entire library, though most of it remained unused for any given specialized cell. Such massive duplicate information would have taken much too long to copy had it been contained within a single book, but spread across many books that were copied in parallel, it opened up a new era of specialized cells working together as the integrated, cooperative team we call an organism.

Even with the gross inefficiency involved in duplicating all the instructions for each different cell type, sufficient informational space still remained in the cells for a guidebook to the developmental order of cell growth and instructions for inter-cellular communication. A gigantic collection of many different types of cells emerged, all with large, identical libraries, but with each cell type following directions from its own special section of the library. As all cells contained the same identical library, they could even trust the reproduction of the organism itself to specialized cells; other, nonreproductive cells wouldn't be cheated because all their information would also get passed on to the next generation.

An initial go at multicellular life, around 600 million years ago, produced a strange array of very flat "pancake" life forms. Then in a second try about 560 million years ago, life hit on the right combination. In an amazingly short time, during the Cambrian explosion, life worked out all the basic forms—the body plans—of multicellular life, although recent research suggests that there may have been some tapping of much deeper, pre-fossil roots. Multicellular organisms developed along three basic lines: fungi, plants, and animals.

Animals with brains know what's going on

Animals are of special interest with respect to information accrual and the further growth of complexity. Some of them developed nerves that gathered information about the location and activities of potential prey or predators, processed this information to formulate an appropriate response, and coordinated rapid muscular movements to implement the response, be it attack or escape. To reduce the expense of the interconnections between information-processing nerves, many animals consolidated these nerves at a single location in a "brain." To minimize distances to nerve-heavy sensors at the front end of animals, brains were usually located in an animal's head.

Short-term memory soon enhanced animal effectiveness: "Is that predator catching up with me? I've been turning right. Is it working? Do I need to turn left?" Some animal brains developed long-term memories, allowing within-lifetime accumulations of useful information about local conditions, as well as past successes and failures. In some animals, the information accumulated during their short lifetimes came to exceed that accumulated genetically by their ancestors over the billions of years since the very first life. This brain-stored information was, of course, lost at each individual's death, while its genetic information, physically transferred to its descendants, continued ever onward.

Animal superorganisms—the pinnacle of complexity

From the viewpoint of ever further increases in complexity, the most important capability of animal brains is their ability to communicate with other brains in members of the same species—to pass information between brains. This has allowed animals to form the large-scale organizations termed "superorganisms." Superorganisms are similar to multi-cellular organisms, but one step up in the hierarchy of evolution. The individual animals within a superorganism take on the roles of the various specialized cells within an organism. In both cases, individual units have to communicate, work together for the good of the whole, follow rules that facilitate cooperation, and accumulate useful information over generations on how best to do all this.

There are some twenty thousand species of animals that biologists classify as superorganisms. Half of these, about ten thousand, are ants, which share a close link with other superorganisms such as the social wasps and highly organized bees. Not closely related to ants are several thousand species of highly successful termites, the social descendants of solitary cockroaches. The members of these various lines of incredibly organized insects are perfect little communists, one and all.

Other mammals, such as wolves, lions, and chimpanzees, certainly form social groups, but they retain considerable selfish individualism, refusing to be subjected entirely to higher-level organization. Thus, packs, prides, and other such groupings are associations, not superorganisms. In a similar vein, we ought to note that ecosystems are not superorganisms. They are associations of sorts, but only very loose ones, without central control or any sacrifice made on the part of various species for the good of the whole ecosystem.

Quarks to supersorganisms—eight levels of complexity

So there we have it: the evolutionary progression of complexity from the Big Bang to animal superorganisms in only 13.7 billion years. It is summarized below as eight hierarchical levels which are arranged from the simplest level to the most complex:

1. Quarks
2. Subatomic particles
3. Atoms
4. Molecules
5. Prokaryotes
6. Eukaryotes
7. Multi-cellular organisms
8. Superorganisms (ants, bees, and termites)

Before proceeding onwards in our story, a false impression this chapter may have created ought to be corrected: that more complex life is somehow better or more successful than simpler life. It is not. Complexity deserves none of these accolades. In fact, life on Earth is primarily bacterial and, except for a brief pre-bacterial episode of complex chemistry, it always has been. Biomass-wise, most bacterial life exists underground—within and between rocks extending some two miles below the Earth's surface. Although subterranean life is thinly spread, its combined mass is staggering—the volume of rock is immense compared with Earth's thin surface area. Mass-wise, surface life is inconsequential, a mere trace on our planet's outer layer.

Even on the surface, bacteria exist in a wider range of environments than other life forms, from boiling hot to freezing cold, extremely acidic to totally alkaline. Microbes live in this wide variety of environments because they have had time to develop the necessary capabilities. Although not more complex, bacterial life is, in this sense, more highly evolved than other life.

Complex surface life doesn't stick around for very long. Bristlecone pines, at a mere four thousand years, are perhaps the longest lived. By comparison, some subterranean microbial life recovered from deep wells is estimated to be several *hundred million* years old and was still living when harvested, albeit at a pace that makes snails seem hypersonic. The life cycle in the deep is geological in duration, beginning near the surface where rock is subducted as continental plates plunge below the crustal surface. Bacteria simply go along for the ride. Soon nutrients become scarce, and bacteria enter a dormant, vegetative state lasting hundreds of millions of years. Eventually, some of these bacteria ride the rocks back to the surface where they resume the frantic lifestyle typical of surface denizens.

It's understandable that surface animals, such as humans, might view plants as the primary providers of food to eat and oxygen to breathe. Animal biomass is, after all, just a minuscule fraction of plant biomass (less than 2%). We are beholden to plants, a view that helps us avoid animal chauvinism. But plants, in turn, are just a tiny fraction of the bacterial biomass, perhaps less than 1%. Plants are not so much primary producers as a minor surface blemish. We must avoid plant chauvinism as well as animal chauvinism if we wish to maintain an unbiased, scientific viewpoint. As animal parasites that feed on plants, we are entirely inconsequential, the least of the minor, the mite on the back of the flea.

As complex beings, however, we have a natural interest in complexity and in how it developed, rare as it might be. The complex fascinates us more than the simple (although some physicists and a few astronomers might demur). We should keep our surface-animal complexity biases in mind, however. Considering their biomass, the number of habitats invaded, and individual organism longevity, bacteria clearly have always been been, and probably always will be, Earth's most successful life.

We turn now to consider the pinnacle of genetic complexity—those wonders of organizational efficiency, the ant colonies.

Chapter 3

ANTS
Jewels of the genetic crown

Go to the ant thou sluggard;
consider her ways, and be wise.
Proverbs 6:6

The ant finds kingdoms in a foot of ground.
Stephen Vincent Benet

Ants—itty bitty, human-cog look-alikes

In the first two chapters of humanity's story we considered, in eight, well-defined hierarchical steps, the rise of complexity from quarks to ants. In each step, lower-level "modules" merged together to form the next, higher-level entity. Central to my scientific version of humanity's story is that modern, civilized *Homo sapiens* have organized themselves as superorganisms, the highest level of complexity, through cultural rather than genetic means. Before we consider ourselves as superorganisms, and the evolutionary path along which we have come, it is instructive to first consider the path of ants, the genetic superorganisms that preceded us by many millions of years. Our story will focus on just a few varieties of ants; superorganisms that are fascinating examples of nature's ingenuity.

Our genetic relationship to ants is remote. We have to go back 600 million years, to the time of the earliest animal life, to find an evolutionary link, a common ancestor between ants and humans. In the long course of evolution, however, we might expect that nature would find similar solutions to the problems involved in organizing thousands or millions of animals into cooperative teams. We would not be disappointed. Such convergence—parallel solutions to organizational problems—is a common theme in evolution throughout nature, and the many parallel solutions to the problem of large-scale coordination between ants and humans are particularly striking.

A typical ant weighs about one ten-millionth as much as a typical human but, collectively, ants are about ten million times more numerous. Thus, surprisingly, their combined weight is roughly the same as our own. Planet-wide, ants account for about 10% of the total land animal biomass; humans make up another 10%. The other ten million or so species of animals share the remaining 80%, although our domesticated animals comprise a hefty portion of this 80%.

Ants are descendants of solitary wasps, insects that lived over 100 million years ago. Over time, subsequent generations of ants led increasingly social lives, with the adult ants working together for the common good and lavishing meticulous care on their young. By 30 million years ago, many species of ants had reached their present form and high degree of biological success. Ants, and the similarly social termites, account for almost three-quarters of the Earth's total insect biomass. In the Amazon jungle, they make up an overwhelming one-third of the total animal biomass. What accounts for the spectacular biological success of the ants (and termites)? How were ants able to banish less-organized, less-social insects to the periphery? Four mutually supportive reasons have been advanced.

Anteese—we smell what we say

Effective inter-ant communication is the first of the four reasons for ant success. Ants signal each other chemically with a vocabulary of some ten to twenty words—much like teenagers do. Separate glands controlled by an ant's miniscule brain secrete each chemical word. Messages of "feed me," "groom me," "follow me," "help me," "alarm", and "emergency evacuation" exist, in addition to those messages pertaining to identification of castes, larvae, and nest mates. These chemical transmissions are supplemented by sound and vibration. The ant's chemical words can, to some extent, be combined to form a variety of phrases. Meanings are explicit; responses are entirely instinctual and uniform.

Success attracts the lazy and the clever in any language, and a few freeloading insects have learned (or rather genetically evolved) the ability to speak "Anteese." Some beetles, for instance, have learned the Anteese phrase for "feed me." The ants, ignoring the appearance of the huge, un-antlike monstrosities sending the message, dutifully regurgitate the requested cuisine. Different ant species secrete various pheromones (chemicals) from their glands, so there are numerous dialects of Antese, perhaps as many as there are separate ant species. Thus, to take advantage of their unwitting benefactors, freeloading beetles must become lingual specialists—which is a small price to pay for a free meal.

Since humans are animals that communicate by sound (and sight), chemical communication seems a strange language to us. With the exception of the persuasive messages that baking bread, the scent of perfume, and our own natural pheromones send, human noses are relatively deaf to chemical messages. Chemistry, however, is the most oft-employed mode of communication for life as a whole. The majority of organisms are simply too small to have eyes, ears, or other proportionally outsized communication devices, let alone the sizable brains required to operate them. Speaking fluently in life's traditional tongue, ants have raised chemical communication to new and impressive heights.

From our human perspective, it's also difficult to understand how ants can, with only a score of simple words, achieve the spectacular coordination that powers their colonies' activities. Their behavior is foreign to us because they accomplish this coordination without the benefit of high-level, central control. Queen ants, far from being the boss ladies, are simply egg-laying machines. Ant factories are entirely decentralized. No timecards, no supervisors, no monthly reports! Its members respond, by way of their stored, mainly hard-wired, behavioral programs, to a combination of inputs—most notably signals from other ants and the physical situation at hand. Such genetically predetermined behavioral repertoires appear quite strange to us, despite the fact that we ourselves have scores of instinctual (hard-wired), primarily unconscious, behavioral repertoires. Unlike the ants, however, our brains are extensively programmed through the bumps and bruises of our own life experiences, not to mention the culturally accumulated dictates of the societies we inhabit.

No matter how efficient, ants are not gifted with intellectual brilliance. There are no Einsteins among them. Individual ants are mere cogs in the colony's machine—genetically pre-programmed to work together harmoniously. A few scientists have suggested that ants resemble six-legged silicon chips. As a species, however, ants have been excellent genetic learners. Over millions of generations, various ant species have acquired the genetic programming necessary to accomplish, in spite of their paltry vocabularies and decentralized "management," amazing feats of large-scale coordination.

Castes—ants are what they eat

The second reason for the ants' success is their caste system of distinctly different but cooperating specialists. A limited number of males are produced seasonally. Their sole task is to spread the genes of the colony to other, newly founded colonies. Few succeed; all quickly die. The largest of the female ants (queens aside) are soldiers, followed in size by an assortment of worker types. Larger workers forage for food and transport it to the nest; smaller workers tend to the young. The soldiers and workers, one and all, are sisters, given that a single queen usually lays all the eggs for an entire colony.

Solitary insects, on the other hand, must accomplish all the sundry soldier, worker, and reproductive functions with a single type of body. Nature is obliged to compromise in order to meet this wide variety of demands. Thus, it isn't surprising that the solitary wasps usually lose if they try to compete directly with their evolutionary descendants, the efficient, specialized, and highly cooperative ants.

Genetic inheritance plays no part in whether an egg becomes a soldier, a worker, or a queen. Instead, ants grow to be, quite literally, what they eat. The type of food they eat and the chemical conditioners spiking their meals determine their body types and careers, i.e., their caste. This approach to differentiation confers on ants the advantage of individual specialization while at the same time allowing various castes of ants to continue together as a single species. Furthermore, this non-genetic approach to differentiation allows for on-the-spot adjustments to the relative proportions of soldiers and various worker types as the colony matures or circumstances change. For instance, if nearly all of the soldiers are lost in a major war, but only few workers perish, the colony can preferentially raise replacement soldiers, certainly a distinct advantage for any army!

Ant redundancy

A third reason for the success of social ants, *vis-à-vis* their solitary relatives, is redundancy—a natural result of the ants' specialization and considerable numbers. Because many multiples of every specialist ant exists, ant colonies can achieve great staying power as a whole. A solitary insect is required to successfully accomplish all life's requisite tasks in series. One error, one stumble over any hurdle along the way, and their game of life is terminated. In the ant world, on the other hand, if one citizen fails to do something properly, another will come along and set it right. Even if an ant dies trying, another will take its place and recommence the effort. The result is that the colony survives. Worker and soldier ants alike are entirely expendable and may live only a few months before being replaced, while queen ants, and the colony itself, endure for years, even decades. Redundancy gives ants an edge over their solitary rivals when they meet head on. Ants can afford to be ludicrously brave in combat. As Bert Holldobler and Edward O. Wilson suggest in their book *Journey to the Ants*, ants are "six-legged kamikazes."

Urban architecture

The fourth and final key to the dominance of many ant species is their permanent and elaborately constructed homes—their architecturally clever "cities." Since many successive generations of ants live in the same structures they are able to maintain their claim to what is, usually, prime real estate—an obvious case of property inheritance. What's more, ants are able to expand and upgrade their ancestral homes over the generations. The substantial size and layout of many ant colonies even allows the occupants to regulate temperature and humidity. By elevating their main entrance, the clever ants not only divert rain run-off, but they also create a chimney that improves air circulation. The hot air expelled by this chimney effect is replaced by cool air drawn in via small holes around the nest's perimeter.

Ecological juggernauts

With all these things going for the social ants, why would any of their solitary competitors remain? The answer is that solitary insects cleverly take advantage of the weaknesses of the ants' organized complexity by learning to make do with limited, transient resources gleaned from the discards. They eke out their livings from the crumbs left by the ants at the colony's periphery.

As anyone from a modern human civilization can appreciate, large, intricately ordered societies do have their downsides. Ant societies are no exception. Colony relocation is difficult or impossible for many ant species, while solitary insects can quickly reposition to another, more favorable location. The utter massiveness of ant colonies requires a substantial base of operations. Furthermore, they take quite some time to reach their full potential. Once well-established however, ant colonies are, as Holldobler and Wilson put it, "ecological juggernauts."

Warfare—no milk–toast Geneva treaties!

There would be no stopping ants if their only competitors were solitary insects, but this is not the case. Ants wage large-scale, highly organized warfare against other ants, as well as termites. Ant wars began when ants first became socially organized insects, and ants have waged war with increasing efficiency and intensity for the past 100 million years. As ants proliferated about the planet, so did the frequency and intensity of their warfare, as they duked it out for increasingly scarce territory and food. The result was an arms race, with the development of ever–more–exotic offenses and inspired defenses. Recent civilized humans aside, no animals have come anywhere close to possessing the large-scale, highly evolved, efficiently organized combat skills of the ants.

Ant offensive warfare is predominantly chemical; no milk-toast Geneva treaties for them! Ants spray poisonous chemicals on their enemies. Some ants have even evolved a specialized soldier caste into chemical bombs. The normally small poison gland on these fighting machines have swollen to tank size. They lumber into the opposing ranks and, quite literally, explode themselves, showering the enemy with poison, in effect becoming suicide bombers.

Ants are also masters of defense. In some species, large soldier ants serve as living doors to the colony's nest using their bodies to block access to all who lack the correct chemical password. Other ant species close their nest entrance with dirt at sunset. When threatened—they simply shut their city's gate.

Might makes right among the ants. The colonies that field the most numerous armies usually win, forcing smaller colonies to less desirable locations or annihilation. But this doesn't always happen. A few species of ants with inherently small colonies have genetically evolved a clever strategy that allows them to hold on to their prime real estate. These species maintain a "rapid reaction force" that normally does nothing but sit around and wait for action. If a single advance scout from a nearby large-colony species is detected, the rapid reaction force is summoned, and they immediately kill the hapless scout. But that's only the beginning. The force then diligently searches the entire area and summarily dispatches any other scouts they find. Because the large ant colonies never hear back from scouts sent into the small colony's territory, they have no reason to go there in force, and the smaller colony remains undetected. We humans also dispatch scouts but, with our central command, would note if any failed to return. Ants, on the other hand, have no such central dispatch system. For the small-colony ants, as with many smaller human societies, constant vigilance is the price of freedom. The deftly conceived strategies and tactics of ant warfare are legion. We humans have added little to this truly ancient art.

While ant warfare is often directed towards other ant species (and also toward the highly organized termites), pitched battles and even long, drawn-out campaigns also occur between different colonies within the same species. The fierce Aztec ants of the Amazon are a case in point. Aztec colonies live in cecropias, plants the size of large cacti. The ants and cecropias have a mutually beneficial relationship—an "I-scratch-your-back-you-scratch-my-back" arrangement. An Aztec colony protects its cecropia from other animals and, in return, the cecropia provides miniature food buds for the ants to eat. All remains peaceful until another Aztec colony tries to move into an already occupied cecropia. This triggers a no-holds-barred, take-no-prisoners campaign that may last for years until, at last, one colony is triumphant and the other totally vanquished. As Eric Hoyt notes, it is a "multi-year saga filled with forced evictions, numerous treacheries, blatant violence, bullying, occasional kidnapping, and pitched battles."

Honeypots—hanging around

A second example can be found in the Arizona desert, home to the honeypot ants. A typical honeypot colony consists of a queen, some twenty thousand sister workers and soldiers, and a couple of thousand specialists called honeypots. The honeypots spend their entire adult lives hanging from the nest's ceiling. During times of plenty, they are fed large quantities of honey-like food and become huge, distended, living storage containers. During lean times, they regurgitate their rich store on command. The honeypot's life may not be an exciting one, but at least they are well fed! There is something to be said for being fat, dumb, and happy. At least they don't have to punch a timeclock to earn a living.

Such concentrations of food wealth are irresistible to other, nearby honeypot colonies. The result is intra-species wars. Opposing ant colonies strut in front of one another, each colony assessing the strength of the other. The ants strive to appear as tall and impressive as possible, even standing atop small pebbles to look larger. If one side seems to be falling behind in the face-off, it calls in reserve soldiers. As long as approximately equal forces are present, no violence ensues, and both sides eventually withdraw. But, if it becomes clear that one side greatly outnumbers the other, the larger colony launches an attack. They chemically mace and charmingly dismember the ants from the smaller colony. The victors then race into the losers' nest to claim their spoils: the honeypots hanging from the ceiling, as well as young grub ants. The honeypots provide a rich source of food for their new masters; the grubs, with careful tending, become workers and soldiers for the victorious colony, swelling its ranks and readying it for further conquest. Neither slavery nor all-out war was invented by humans.

Ants are formidable predators, using their massed numbers and organizational skills to overpower animals many times their own size, hack them apart, and transport easily managed pieces back to the nest as food. Army ants are legendary—millions of miniature wolves on the prowl. A hunted animal can only hope to flee the marauding ant columns. A beset animal can only hope for quick death.

Ant herders

Some ant species are primarily carnivorous while others, such as the Aztec, prefer rich plant fruits. Whether carnivores or frugivores, ants are, by necessity, comparatively rare because they are eating off the top of the food chain. Hunters and picky gatherers living near the top of the food chain can never be numerous. Ecologist Paul Colinvaux encapsulated this fundamental ecological fact in the title of his delightful book *Why Big Fierce Animals Are Rare*. Ants simply cannot digest the more plentiful, but coarse, plant material. Although most ants depend on meat hunting and fruit gathering, the most advanced species have gone much further by engaging in what may, without exaggeration, be called herding and farming. They utilize other animals to eat plants for them, thus tapping into the otherwise inaccessible coarse plant material at the base of the food chain.

Plants utilize about 2% of the sunlight that falls on them to grow and sustain themselves. However, only about 10% of the energy captured by plants is available as food for animals, so the biomass of herbivores can only be about one-tenth the biomass of the plants they feed on. Similarly, about 90% of the energy herbivores obtain from plants is used for moving about and maintaining themselves. Only the remaining 10% is available as food for the carnivores, another step up the food chain.

In short, the rare carnivores feed on the more numerous herbivores, which eat the widespread plants that soak up the sun's energy. We may admire carnivorous hunters for their skill and cunning, but it is herders and especially farmers, both ant and human, who have always had the ecologically bestowed advantage of tapping the bottom of the food chain. This has allowed them to be many instead of few.

Certain animals, such as aphids and various caterpillars, are capable of directly eating tough plants, but neither ants nor humans are equipped to digest such course cellulose in its raw form. Both ruminants (such as cows) and termites utilize bacteria in their stomachs or guts to digest such plentiful plant roughage. This is an "internal" approach. Some of the most successful ants rely on a more sophisticated "external approach": they use domesticated animals or fungi to process the otherwise indigestible course cellulose. However, such control of other species is not easy to achieve. Ants won their remarkable control over other species through the efficient cooperation of specialized castes and the massed force of thousands or even millions of ants living together in colonies.

A number of plant-eating insects, such as aphids, mealybugs, and leafhoppers, excrete a by-product—honeydew—which is, water aside, 90% sugar. One insect's waste is another's food; ants and other insects eat honeydew with relish. Killing the geese that lay the golden eggs, carnivorous beetles simply eat the aphids—honeydew and all. As a result, several species of aphids have evolved a special arrangement with ants: if the ants protect the aphids from predators, the aphids will serve up their honeydew exclusively to their saviors. Some aphids have even developed ant-friendly honeydew storage systems, releasing their accumulated honeydew only when appropriately triggered by a "milking" ant. In a number of cases, this ant-aphid symbiotic relationship has become quite permanent. Over time, some aphids have lost any natural defenses and can only survive as the wards of their protective ant lords. Such aphids are truly domesticated. These herding ants have, by proxy, become herbivores, achieving large numbers by finding a clever key to an immense source of energy. By tapping the bottom of the food chain, they have, as a species, become numerous instead of rare.

For their part, ants not only protect their aphid "cattle," they also periodically move their stock to greener pastures. Ants gently carry the aphids in their jaws to a suitable species of plant, where they deposit their charges on the appropriate part of the plant for the particular developmental stage of each individual aphid. At night, ants move their aphid cattle into the safety of special barn-like chambers in the ants' own nest. In cold climates, some ants go so far as to bring aphids into their own homes for the entire winter, giving their aphid livestock the same loving care as their own ant young. Come spring, the ants move their aphids out to pasture again.

Some ants have become totally dependent on aphids as their food source, living almost entirely off their herd's honeydew except for selectively eating a few of the ever-growing aphid herd, a process human herders call "thinning." When young queen ants fly off to start a new colony, they go equipped with a dowry in the form of a few aphids. Holldobler and Wilson term this "homesteading with pregnant cow in tow."

While most herder ants operate from a fixed location, colonies of one species in the Malaysian rain forest, *Hupoclinea cuspidatus*, are true nomadic herders. Always on the move, they take their entire herd of approximately five thousand mealybugs with them wherever they go.

Ant gardening

Aphid and mealybug herding is just one of two sophisticated strategies ants use to access readily available leaves and other plant material their digestive systems can't handle. The second is a form of mushroom gardening. Instead of using horse manure to grow mushrooms, gardening ants mulch up vast quantities of leaves on which they grow nutritious mushroom-like fungus. Other species of farming ants use dead insect bodies and other organic material to grow fungi.

The leaf-munching ant gardeners are various species of fungus-growers that live exclusively in the jungles of the Western Hemisphere. The most famous of these are the leafcutters, commonly called parasol ants because the pieces of leaf they carry over their heads resemble miniature umbrellas. Leafcutters build mammoth, fixed-base colonies, each with up to five million inhabitants. They remove several tons of soil to create underground tunnels and chambers. The leafcutters' agricultural operations resemble manufacturing production lines, passing the product from one stage to the next. A different size of specialized worker handles each stage. Henry Ford would have approved, had he visited such a colony.

In a typical leafcutter colony, the largest ants are the soldiers, who stand guard over the whole process. The largest workers are the leaf-cutting transport ants. Their massive jaws effortlessly clip out sections of the toughest leaves. These clippings rain down to the jungle floor. Others of the same caste sling them over their backs for the journey home, bearing their burdens without difficulty, even though each standard leaf segment weighs three times as much as the ant that carries it. Long columns, sometimes ten ants abreast, mark the transport highway. The processing of these leaf segments for edibility begins in underground garden chambers, where smaller ants chop the harvest into tiny pieces. Still smaller castes crush the leaves and shape them into miniature pellets. At this point an altogether different caste takes over and seeds the pellets with a specially domesticated fungus originally brought in by the founding queen as a dowry. Finally, the tiniest caste of all repeatedly weeds the gardens of unwanted species of fungi and other unwelcome guests and harvests full-grown fungi for the entire colony to eat. Members of the largest caste, the soldiers, weigh some three hundred times more than the members of the smallest caste, even though all castes are genetic sisters. These enormous size differences are highly adaptive—fostering a more efficient colony. The large leafcutter and transport ants are much too big to move within the narrow confines of the smaller garden passageways, while the smallest gardener ants have nowhere near the strength required to sever a tough leaf, let alone carry it home.

The ancestors of modern leafcutters began their fungus gardening roughly 25 million years ago. At that time, workers were all one size, and the process lacked its modern production-line efficiency. Ants harvested the tender young fungi before they entered the less edible spore stage to reproduce themselves, requiring the ants to propagate the fungi clonally, i.e., suppressing the spore stage in the fungus reproductive cycle. In time, the domesticated fungi lost their ability to produce spores, becoming totally dependent on ant gardeners for their propagation. Recent DNA analysis of these domesticated fungi indicates that leafcutter ants have been growing the same lines of fungi for over 20 million years. Johnny-come-lately human gardeners please take note!

About 2.5 million years ago, the Isthmus of Panama rose above sea-level and reconnected North and South America after a long separation. This geological event, as we will note later, may also have been responsible for the major shift in world climate that might have triggered our own hominid line's rise from obscure chimpdom. Leafcutter ants, which originated in South America, moved across the isthmus into Central America. Some 2.5 million years later, two of the planet's most successful farming animals, leafcutters and humans, finally met each other in the corn and bean fields of Mexico, when leafcutters raided the New World's first human agricultural plots. Squaring off, farmer-to-farmer, humans generally came in second best against the invader ants.

While only a few species of leafcutter ants exist—all in the New World—their numbers are legion. Not only do they remove vast quantities of vegetation from American jungles, they also appropriate billions of dollars worth of crops from human farmers each year. Leafcutters are the primary herbivore of the American tropics; a single colony consumes as much vegetation as a cow. When it comes to sophisticated, large-scale organizations, the leafcutter ants are among the most brilliant jewels of the genetic crown.

Chapter 4

CHIMPANZEES

Masters of Machiavellian intrigue

Chimpanzees, those amazing creatures
who can teach us so much about ourselves
even while we become fascinated by them
in their own right

Jane Goodall

The roots of politics are older than humanity.

Frans de Waal

Of animals, brains, and culture

So far, we have traced the evolution of complexity, one layer at the time, from the quarks created during the Big Bang to, on our local planet, ant superorganisms—all in just the eight hierarchical steps enumerated at the end of Chapter 2. We must backtrack now, albeit a measly 600 million years, to the Cambrian explosion to pick up the thread of animal life that led to animals with brains larger than the miniscule ganglions of the ants.

Animals with significant-sized brains lead lives filled with fast-paced decisions—many of life-or-death import. In addition to their endowment of genetic information, patiently gathered over millions of years, animals with brains are able to accumulate, within the short space of their own lifetimes, substantial information on local conditions. They draw on this individually accumulated within-lifetime "stored brain information," in conjunction with their inherited genetic "wisdom," to make informed decisions

Given the often fatal penalty for erroneous decisions, one might reason that all animals would develop the largest possible brains in order to swiftly process all inputs and fully consider the myriad of possibilities in every situation. This doesn't happen because large brains are costly. The neurons that comprise an animal's brain cells require a great deal of metabolic support. Unlike muscle cells, which burn little energy while at rest, brain cells are always on the go, continuously burning calories at a prodigious rate. On average, brain cells burn about ten times as much energy as muscle cells. And, the larger the brain, the more food needed to fuel it. The more food an animal needs, the greater its exposure to danger while finding food.

The primary function of an animal's brain is to orient it with respect to the world, allowing it to make rapid, yet reasonably accurate decisions. Brains automatically make low-level decisions, such as retracting a paw from a hot stone, without the need for much thought. But higher level decisions, such as mate choice or the appropriate way to interact with one's neighbor, require significant thought.

In addition to individual learning, social animals with overlapping generations and sizeable brains can culturally transfer limited amounts of information from one generation to the next. Such transfer opened a second channel besides DNA for the accumulation and refinement, across the generations, of information on how cooperative social animals might best survive and prosper. Although for years we thought culture was strictly a human prerogative, scientists have increasingly given animals credit for having at least a limited cultural capacity.

Thus it should come as no surprise that our closest living relatives in the animal world, two species of chimpanzee, are noted for their cultural traditions. This similarity between chimpanzees and us is due, logically enough, to descent from a recent common ancestor that, presumably, was also culturally inclined. Perhaps, as suggested by the catchy title of Jared Diamond's book, our species is just *The Third Chimpanzee*.

You can't choose your relatives

Common chimpanzees primarily eat fruit—nearly two-thirds of their diet. They also consume tender young leaves, seeds, and insects. Not strict vegetarians, chimps occasionally savor morsels of meat from the small animals that the male chimps cooperatively hunt. About half their days are spent feeding and the rest are spent traveling to new trees, grooming, and various other activities. Muscular—much stronger than humans—chimpanzees can climb trees with ease. They are quite comfortable traveling a hundred feet above the ground, even though they prefer to traverse long distances via knuckle-walking on the ground.

Pan troglodytes, the common chimpanzee, comes immediately to mind when chimpanzees are mentioned, but there is another, lesser known species, *Pan paniscus,* the bonobo. Bonobos are occasionally called pygmy chimpanzees because they are slightly smaller than their better-known relatives. The bonobo's most striking feature is its human-like appearance. *Paniscus* is flat-faced, often maintains an upright stance, and engages in face-to-face sex—uncommon in the animal kingdom. Bonobos are less aggressive than common chimpanzees and do not appear to hunt.

That these two species of chimpanzee are our closest relatives is no longer in doubt. DNA analysis shows that we three species all descended from a common ancestor who lived some six million years ago. We share over 98% of our genes in common with chimpanzees. Gorillas and orangutans, our next closest relatives, are more DNA-distant from both us and chimpanzees. Put another way, humans, not gorillas or orangutans, are the closest relatives of the common chimpanzees and bonobos. When Linnaeus—the Swedish classifier of life—lumped the great apes (chimpanzees, gorillas, and orangutans) together, but placed humans in a separate category, he made a zoological classification error (although it was probably a smart move politically). We now know that we are actually a great ape and, perhaps, should be classified, as Jarod suggest, as a third species of chimpanzee—*Pan sapiens.*

Jane Goodall—chimpanzees like us

Many scientists, however, have long held that we are worlds apart from our two sister species in terms of behavior. Decades ago, anthropologist Louis Leakey realized that our understanding of chimpanzee behavior, based as it was on observations made in zoos and other captive conditions, was inadequate as a basis of comparison to our own behavior. True understanding, he reasoned, would come only by observing how our closest relatives actually lived in the wild. To this end, he arranged, in the early 1960s, for Jane Goodall to observe a group of wild chimpanzees in East Africa. Observe she did—for over three decades!

Goodall was not trained as a scientist before beginning her observations. She didn't know that it was scientifically improper to give individual animals names, let alone to invoke any human-style emotions when explaining their behavior. For most animals, such anthropomorphism (projection of human motivations onto animals) would indeed have been a serious scientific error. In the case of chimpanzees, however, it was a stroke of good luck. When studying animals other than chimpanzees, we often credited them with too many human attributes. With chimpanzees, by contrast, we had, until Goodall came along, tended to distance ourselves from them more than was justified—they were, after all, just animals, and we were above the animals. As subsequent research has amply demonstrated, however, it's safe to assume that chimpanzees are similar to humans in many ways.

One of humanity's longest-standing claims to uniqueness is that only we are self-conscious. However, Goodall's field observations suggested that chimpanzees are self-conscious too. For those desiring a more formal scientific study under controlled conditions, Gordon Gallup conducted, in the late 1960s, his famous mirror-and-red-spot experiment. He provided various animals with mirrors, enlisting those that could view their own image without panic in his clever experiment. While the animals were anesthetized, Gallup surreptitiously painted a harmless red spot on their foreheads. On awakening and looking in a mirror, individuals of only three species immediately reached to their foreheads to feel the strange red spot they observed on themselves in the mirror. These species were chimpanzees, orangutans, and humans. (A sign-language-trained captive gorilla, Koko, later did the same thing.) Gallup suggested that this was not just a case of apes figuring out how a mirror works.

Several species of monkeys are able to do that, using mirrors to find hidden food. Rather, apes identify themselves in mirrors because they, like us, have a concept of self.

Jane Goodall's classic book *In the Shadow of Man*, based on her first decade of chimpanzee observations, reads like a biography of the Roosevelts or Kennedys—one soon forgets that the characters are not human. The strong family bonds, lifelong friendships, rivalries, and political intrigues are all endearingly human. Sadly, Goodall's early portrait of the happy, playful, loving chimpanzees did not survive the test of time. Chimpanzees are not, in fact, entirely good-natured. Jane Goodall's continued observations eventually revealed a darker side: the psychotically jealous baby killer; the cold, ruthless murders, one by one, of a breakaway subgroup. Her second popular book, *Through a Window: My Thirty Years with the Chimpanzees of Gombe*, rather graphically reveals these unpleasant, but still hauntingly human facets of chimpanzee behavior. The common chimpanzees now appear to form Mafia-like families, with occasional murders and sadistic beatings contrasting sharply with their usually warm, affectionate natures.

Chimpanzee politics

Franz de Waal observed, recorded, and analyzed the social interactions in a sizable colony of common chimpanzees that lived relatively undisturbed on an island in a zoo in Belgium. He found that the social interactions between chimpanzees were politically astute. Brute strength took a back seat to political finesse. These observations of chimpanzees suggested that their large brains resulted from a within-species arms race of sorts, a game of intricate social chess. Chimpanzees had evolved Machiavellian intelligence. The rank of an individual chimpanzee does not correlate directly with physical power. Chimps build up a network of relatives and friends over a lifetime. Connections count in chimpanzee society, so the alpha male is not always the largest or strongest.

The alpha male is typically an astute politician, currying favor with female supporters by playing with and even kissing their babies. Apparently, presidential politics have been around for a long time. Chimpanzees are good at remembering who owes them favors and to whom they owe favors. Keeping track of constantly shifting alliances in a group of forty or fifty chimpanzees is a major intellectual accomplishment—one these animals have evolved large brains to handle. And, like us, they love soap operas.

Chimpanzees are, as de Waal suggests in the title of his recent book, inherently *Good Natured*. In spite of their occasional murderous acts—discovered by Goodall—they are, in the main, nonviolent, faithful, caring, and loving to family and friends. They usually settle conflicts within their community by prompt reconciliations accompanied by grooming, hugs and, in the case of the bonobos, sex.

Chimpanzees have well-developed mental models of the personalities, emotions, and motives of other chimpanzees in their group, keeping careful account of the complex and ever-shifting interrelationships among those with whom they live day-to-day. Chimpanzees are not only self-conscious, but are always projecting ahead: if I do this, he will do that, and then she will join in. Such thoughts are mental models of social cause and effect, i.e., theories of mind.

Sticks and stones

Early on, Goodall observed a behavior heretofore thought to be uniquely human: the manufacture and use of tools. Tool-making chimpanzees at Gombe broke off long stems, clipped off side leaves and excess length, and then inserted these tools into the entrances of termite nests. Pausing to allow the termites to attack this stem intruder into their nest, they slowly and carefully withdrew their tools, now teeming with protein. They then quickly passed the stick through their mouths, skimming off termites and swallowing them with obvious satisfaction. Guaranteed fresh! This tool-making, tool-using tradition is passed from one generation to the next. Subsequent observations by other primatologists have revealed that tool traditions are not unique to the Gombe chimps, although specific traditions vary from one band to the next. Chimpanzees in different groups also use leaves as tools in various ways. In their hands, leaves become umbrellas, sponges for water, or personal hygiene napkins.

The most amazing cultural tradition of all is that of the nut-cracking chimpanzees of the Tai forest in West Africa. Discovered by Christophe Boesch, a Swiss primatologist, these common chimpanzees eat a plentiful nut that in season provides over half their calories. The shell is so hard it can only be broken open with a stone hammer. It takes great skill to avoid smashing the nut to an inedible pulp of shell and meat, not to mention smashing one's fingers. The stone must precisely strike a nut carefully held between two fingers in the slight depression of a wooden anvil-like log. Mothers patiently "teach" their children how to crack nuts, step by step. First, they leave nuts and a hammer stone near an anvil to play with. Then, as their children get older, they encourage them to try cracking nuts, keeping them well supplied. If the young chimps use an inappropriate technique, the mothers, on very rare occasions, have even been seen to interrupt and demonstrate the correct technique. The nut cracking skill is eventually learned, but it takes several years, hundreds of practice sessions, and some bruised knuckles, before young chimpanzees finally get the hang of it.

How long have the Tai chimpanzees been nut crackers? Is it truly a cultural tradition? Boesch points out that in the Tai forest, chimpanzees on one side of the Sassandra River crack nuts, while those on the other side, where the nuts are just as plentiful, do not. During the last ice age, which occurred about 17 thousand years ago, the already greatly reduced jungle broke up into isolated pockets. The nut-cracking tradition apparently spread from a single pocket of the jungle as wetter weather allowed the jungle to expand but was blocked from further expansion by the Sassandra River.

Kanzi—a bonobo for all seasons

In addition to being studied in natural settings, chimpanzees have now been studied extensively under artificial, but often pleasant and enriching environments. Washoe, a common chimp, was raised by the Gardeners in their home in Reno, Nevada, in a manner similar to a human child's upbringing. Because the vocal tracts of chimpanzees are not capable of human speech, the Gardeners taught Washoe American Sign Language. Washoe was (perhaps arguably) able to learn about a hundred signs, mainly objects and verbs. To the Gardeners, it was clear that Washoe had acquired the capability of speech. A few vocal critics (no pun intended) remained dubious, however, suggesting the Gardner's were giving Washoe too much credit.

Bonobos have also been observed extensively, both in their natural setting south of the Congo river in Central Africa and in a large colony at the San Diego Zoo. Bonobos look strikingly human because, like us, they retain many juvenile facial features into adulthood; these are the juvenile features of our common ancestor. The facial features of a chimpanzee, by contrast, change as they age so that they look strikingly different as adults. Unlike common chimpanzees, bonobo males and females are nearly equal in size, indicative of their egalitarian society. Following the dictate "make love, not war," bonobo political life has a decided, and to us prudish humans, embarrassingly blatant sexual slant to it. Sex lubricates the workings of their peaceful societies.

At the Yerkes Primate Center near Atlanta, primatologists Sue Savage-Rumbaugh and Diane Rumbaugh initiated language instruction of both common chimpanzees and bonobos. Instead of American Sign Language, they communicated by way of special computer keyboards and video displays and also spoken English. The chimpanzees responded via keyboard or action. Their efforts succeeded only marginally at first. Then, one day, while Sue was patiently giving language lessons to a slow-learning bonobo mother, the two-year-old son, Kanzi, shocked Sue with a demonstration of his heretofore-unsuspected skill of understanding spoken English. He tapped out meaningful answers on his mother's portable keyboard. Like human children everywhere, he had easily learned a new language, while his over-the-hill mother, the intended student, had great difficulty in doing so. Kanzi went on to become an effective English listener (as far as such things go among apes), understanding 150 words by the age of six. This is comparable to the linguistic skills of a two-year-old human.

A bonobo for all seasons, Kanzi became the only ape known to fashion stone tools, as opposed to just selecting appropriate stones. Nicholas Toth, an anthropologist who specializes in making stone tools in a manner thought similar to that of our early ancestors, taught Kanzi the rudiments of this ancient art. Kanzi, with considerable instruction and encouragement, was brought closer to being human than any other animal has been.

Gorillas in the mist and orangutans in Eden

Louis Leakey not only sent Jane Goodall to observe chimpanzees in the wild, he also sent Diane Fossey to observe gorillas, and Birute Galdikas to observe orangutans. Leakey felt women made better, more patient observers than did men. He also thought women would appear less threatening to the male-dominated great ape societies. Diane Fossey's book, *Gorillas in the Mist,* was made into a movie not long after her untimely death. She was murdered, some thought, in retaliation for her zealous protection of her gorillas against unlawful poachers.

Birute Galdikas, who observed orangutans deep in the Borneo Jungle for decades, recently wrote *Reflections of Eden*. She found that orangutans make tools in the wild, are very handy with human tools, and share many traits with the other great apes and humans.

Louis Leakey's "three angels" (Goodall, Fossey, and Galdikas), along with dozens of other hard-working primatologists from around the world, have revolutionized our view of humanity, giving it a distinctly more scientific, evolutionary flavor. It seems likely that much of what we have only recently considered uniquely human is, in fact, traceable to the common ancestor of all great apes some twelve million years ago. Deep roots indeed!

What should we conclude from this? Are we a third species of chimpanzee? Anatomically and genetically, the answer is an unreserved "Yes!" Behaviorally, too, we are more similar to our chimpanzee kinsfolk—and them to us—than previously thought. All three of us are self-reflecting, politically astute, tool-making, social beings capable of symbolic communication. Of the three species, however, two now face extinction, while the third dominates the planet. How did this come about?

PART II

How Did We Come To Be?
Cultural evolution takes command

Human history is a story of cultural takeover.
Kevin Kelly

Far from being the descendants of gods,
we emerge at the summit of an arduous ascent.
Hubert Reeves

Chapter 5

HOMINIDS
The chimpanzees who were thrown to the lions

When humans first appear,
they are already holding tools.
Bruce Mazlish

Progress, man's distinctive mark alone,
not God's, and not the beasts': God is, they are,
man partly is and wholly hopes to be.
Robert Browning

Eastside Story

How did it happen that a few chimpanzee-like primates become the planet's most well organized animal in a mere six million years, beating the ants at their own game? Why is it that humans have prospered while extinction now threatens our closest genetic relatives, the true chimps who were blessed with the enduring jungles of Central and West Africa?

French anthropologist Yves Coppens, with witty deference to the American composer George Gershwin, dubbed his portrayal of the first act of our hominid adventure the *Eastside Story*. In a single phrase, Coppens neatly captured the essence of three outcomes of a single geological event: the timing of our evolutionary split from the chimpanzees about six million years ago, the physical location of the earliest hominid fossils in eastern Africa, and the present habitat of chimpanzees in central and western Africa. This geological event, which began nearly eight million years ago, was the formation of the Rift Valley and its associated mountains, as one tectonic plate sank beneath the surface and pushed up another. Coppens suggested that these high mountains and deep valleys—which extend for thousands of miles in a north-south direction—effectively split the Earth's chimpanzee population in two, leaving the main body west of the mountains and a smaller body to the east. Furthermore, because the prevalent wind direction in this part of Africa is from west to east, these new mountains cast a rain shadow over eastern Africa. The result: the wet west remained jungle while the drying east became scattered woodland.

The gradual deforestation of eastern Africa accelerated dramatically six million years ago when Antarctica arrived, again due to shifting tectonic plates, at its present position straddling the South Pole. Winter snowfalls failed to completely melt during the frigid summers, so not only did the snow-covered ground reflect the summer sun's heat back into space—further deepening the chill—it also enabled immense sheets of ice to accumulate. As Antarctic ice increasingly locked up the oceans, sea levels dropped. When they fell below the lowest point in the Strait of Gibraltar, the Atlantic no longer flowed into the Mediterranean, replacing water lost to evaporation. Soon the Mediterranean dried up, as we are able to deduce from the deep deposits of salt recently discovered and dated to six million years ago.

The forest floors in the dense Western jungles continued to receive little sunlight, hence providing scant forage for ground-dwelling herbivores and, in turn, limited herbivore flesh for fierce ground-dwelling carnivores. The paucity of lions and their ilk was, presumably, beneficial for the westside chimpanzees, and the chimpanzees of central and western Africa never lost their tree-dense home altogether. Though the cool, dry climate significantly reduced their habitat's extent, sufficient jungle remained throughout this era for them to continue evolving their chimpanzee ways; they never left their Garden of Eden.

On the other hand, the progressively cooler, drier climate that emerged east of the Rift Mountains transformed the jungles there into scattered woodlands, and the many open, sunlit patches encouraged the growth of forage. Herbivores soon abounded, as did the predators that ate them—not such good news for our eastside hominid ancestors.

Marathon walking

The climate in eastern Africa changed in a patchy manner, providing a kaleidoscope of diverse habitats; some drier, others higher, while still others remained more wooded. This patch quilt of small, isolated, and varied environments was ideally suited for the emergence of new species. American paleontologist Elizabeth Vrba established that numerous new animal species appeared immediately after a significant extinction in eastern Africa five million years ago. She noted, for instance, that a number of new species of antelope appeared in eastern Africa at this time. Vrba termed this rapid change in fauna a "turnover pulse," associating it with the dramatic climatic changes.

For our hominid ancestors, who were adapted to jungle life, this eastern scenario was not so fortunate. They faced their first Darwinian crisis. Their immediate challenge: getting enough to eat, since obtaining sufficient fruit within a contiguous strand of trees became difficult. Chimpanzees are ill equipped to travel in the open over protracted distances on the ground because they knuckle-walk—which is an ambling, rather inefficient mode of travel. Bipedal locomotion, on the other hand, is more energy efficient, allowing one to cover greater distances on the same food calories. As the east-African climate dried out and the gaps between groves widened, hominids desperately needed efficient ground travel. Evolution selected hominid bipedalism and marathon walking soon became an everyday event. Obtaining one's next meal has always been of evolutionary importance!

Mad dashes to the nearest tree

Although bipedal locomotion is considerably faster than knuckle-walking, it's not as fast as the four-legged locomotion of carnivores. Thus, early hominids faced their second Darwinian challenge: avoiding getting eaten as they crossed the open spaces between groves of trees. As paleontologist Steven Stanley wryly suggested, "Anthropologists should devote more attention to what ate our ancestors as opposed to what our ancestors ate." Stanley suggested that the woodlands became "killing fields" every night, with those animals incapable of outrunning predators either spending the night in trees or burrowing underground. Our ancestors naturally chose the trees, probably sleeping in nests similar to those made by chimpanzees and orangutans. To this day, tree houses give us that secure, sheltered feeling, while lions still strike terror in our chimpanzee souls.

Although the open spaces between groves were safer during the day than at night, lions, hyenas, and wild dogs still lurked about. The abrupt appearance of such carnivores and the heart-pounding race for the nearest trees must have been an almost daily occurrence of terror for our early hominid ancestors. Sprinting was, perhaps, our second track and field event, right after marathon walking. Slower hominids were naturally the first to be caught, food for predators while the rest climbed to safety—hence the ancient saying, "I may be slow but I'm faster than you!" It's not surprising that the earliest-known hominids, although they were bipedal, retained their ability to climb trees; as citizens of two worlds, field and forest, they necessarily led double lives.

There is no doubt about our early bipedality. Fossils such as Lucy, discovered by Donald Johnson, bear indisputable witness. Lucy is estimated to have lived over three million years ago. Equally ancient witnesses are the footprints of two hominids in freshly fallen ash from a Rift Mountain volcano. Gently wetted by rain, these ashen footprints subsequently turned to stone. Mary Leaky and Paul Abell discovered them in Laetoli, Tanzania, in 1978. A second, smaller hominid was, for the most part, stepping in the footprints of a larger, leading hominid—most likely a child following his or her mother.

New and improved sticks and stones

Chimpanzees used simple tools, but bipedality freed hominid hands to more efficiently make tools and to greatly expand their use. Although stone tools weren't evident until the beginning of the hominid artifactual record some 2.5 million years ago, it is likely that our predecessors used non-lithic tools much earlier. We haven't found these earlier artifacts because it is likely that hominids initially made tools of wood and other perishable materials or simply selected naturally shaped stones. In either case, no record would have survived. A good case can be made that significant changes in the hand bones of early hominids prior to

2.5 million years ago—changes that accompanied our so-called power grip—were driven by extensive tool making and tool use.

Although early hominids remained frugivores to some extent—as deduced from the telltale scratches on their teeth from fruit eating—their subsequently enlarged molars suggest that their diets increasingly included seeds and tubers, presumably gathered or excavated with stick tools. Such roughage requires the grinding power of the large molar teeth which soon appeared in the fossil record.

Thrown to the lions

For millions of years, we hominids changed only modestly. We coasted along in our scattered woodlands while our sister species, the common chimpanzees and bonobos, did their jungle thing in the west. Even though our ancestors achieved bipedality and a modest increase in tool use, there was still little hint of any advance beyond that of slightly glorified woodland chimpanzees.

For the better part of those millions of years, there also was no hint of increased brain size. Perhaps brains didn't expand because we weren't doing anything different except, perhaps, walking farther between fruit trees—not exactly an intellectually demanding task! And brains, as mentioned earlier, are expensive; they consume disproportionate amounts of energy. Our chimpanzee-sized brains were already extraordinarily large, as mammals go, presumably having evolved to handle sophisticated social interactions.

Most chimpanzee brain growth necessarily occurs prenatally, because once born, infant chimps must be mature enough to cling for dear life to their tree-climbing mothers. Early hominid mothers similarly needed all four "hands" to climb trees on occasion (lions nipping at their heels) and, obviously, could not be holding infants while doing so.

Our era of stasis came to an abrupt halt some 2.5 million years ago, when disaster struck. A precipitous drop in the Earth's temperature brought on the Ice Ages. Although spared the ice, cold and dry go together and, as a result, the climate of Africa was dramatically transformed. In central and western Africa, the jungles shrank to less than 20% of their former area.

With only a few disconnected pockets remaining, our jungle-dependent chimpanzee relatives had a close brush with extinction. In an already-dry eastern Africa, the change was even more severe. Savannas replaced woodlands. Our ancestors lost their indispensable trees. Without trees for their nightly shelter, our hominid ancestors were, literally, thrown to the lions.

Although theories abound as to what brought on the Ice Ages 2.5 million years ago, we'll limit ourselves to two, one geological, the other astronomical. The geological theory suggests that the Pacific-Atlantic sea connection across Central America, which had existed for millions of years, closed when the Isthmus of Panama rose—sort of a reverse Panama Canal. The resultant change in ocean circulation increased cloudiness over northern America and Europe, reflecting more sunlight back into space. This allowed the buildup of a Northern Hemisphere ice cap to complement the one already in place in Antarctica.

The other, astronomical theory, postulates that the orbit and tilt of the Earth changes over time. More importantly, it also suggests that our sun, far from having a constant energy output, is a variable star. On occasion, its normally high level of activity (evidenced by sun spots) falls off, its spots slowly vanish, and its energy flow lessens. The Earth cools. This happened briefly, for example, during the Little Ice Age six hundred years ago; in response, the Thames froze over solid, the Vikings were forced to abandon Greenland, and European population fell as food production plummeted. After almost a hundred-year absence, sunspots reappeared, and temperatures soon returned to normal. Was this disappearing act a fluke or an indication of normal stellar behavior? We have reason to believe that stars similar to our sun periodically dampen their fires, so to speak, because we have seen this happen on many sun-like stars as their starspots turn off, just as our own sun's did during the Little Ice Age.

Whatever the cause of the Ice Ages, as temperatures plummeted and rain became scarce, much of eastern Africa became grassy savanna. Here and there, small disconnected pockets of woodland lingered on for a while, although they continued to shrink in size. Another Vrba turnover pulse of extinctions swept eastern Africa, and it's easy to envision the growing desperation of hominids trapped in the shrinking woodland islands, their main source of food—fruit—rapidly disappearing while, at the same time, their safe havens from predators were vanishing.

Dig for potatoes or eat steak?

With their sustaining fruit trees quickly fading, our ancestors faced their third Darwinian crisis. Like their second one, it was an ideal setup for evolutionary experimentation. Under severe environmental pressure, hundreds of small groups of hominids, each on its own dwindling woodland isle, battled for survival. Most groups were doubtless driven to extinction by the lack of their staple food, fruit; as hunger weakened them, the lions picked them off. But two hominid lines evolved into something new, and survived, each by the virtue of its own unique strategy. Darwin would have been pleased.

Both strategies relied on eating less fruit and more fibrous material, such as vegetables and tubers. We infer this shift in diet from changes in fossilized hominid teeth. One of the two groups, *robustus*, simply took the coarser diet much further than the other, their teeth growing into ever more efficient grinders, their jaws into powerful crushers. Because the vegetables this group consumed were less nutritious than fruit, they had to eat more, becoming veritable feeding machines. Their increasingly thick skulls sprouted a sagittal crest that supported the attachment of ever more powerful jaw muscles. They evolved into bipedal gorilla-like forms, vegetarians that ate immense quantities of coarse food. Vrba noted that these hominids simply "chewed their way out of trouble." These browsing, digging hominids fared reasonably well on the edges of the eastern African savanna for quite some time.

The second successful strategy for coping with the disappearing fruit trees was altogether different. Instead of coming to rely on massive amounts of coarse vegetables, hominids in this group, *Homo habilis*, began to eat anything that didn't eat them first—the savannas were, after all, filled with game. This dietary shift was not entirely out of the blue; jungle chimpanzees had always enjoyed the occasional meaty morsel. Under the stress of fruit scarcity, this second group, including our ancestors, simply ate more meat than before. Again, the teeth are revealing. While the molar teeth of *robustus* continued to enlarge until they essentially became grinding millstones, the molars of the meat eaters reversed their growth and became smaller. Meat has more concentrated energy than vegetables, and is a rich source of protein, with a natural balance of all the essential amino acids. Furthermore, meat is more nutritionally compact than vegetables, so it takes less time to eat; meat eaters don't have to spend most of their waking hours munching.

Our ancestors probably obtained most of their meat by scavenging, not by hunting. Scavenging on the open savanna, competing with buzzards, jackals, hyenas, and lions, was an extraordinarily gutsy move for these reclusive, bashful apes. Such bravery could have only resulted from the extreme desperation stemming from the disappearance of their beloved fruit trees. We can clearly envision a group of hominids defying their fate in one of the last woodland bastions surrounded by vast stretches of treeless, deadly savanna. Year by year, the trees grew sparser, and of necessity, meat and vegetables replaced fruit. Hominids spent increasing time on the savanna, creeping farther and farther from the closest trees. Over generations, natural selection favored those most alert and responsive to the demands of their new environment. By the time the last trees disappeared, our ancestors were ready to survive on the open savanna.

Children of the Ice Age

As the trees dwindled, compelling reasons to develop an even larger brain finally presented themselves. Larger hominid groups enjoyed an obvious survival advantage on the open savanna; a hundred stone-throwing, screaming hominids must have given even lions pause. But keeping larger groups glued together socially took larger brains. The number of interactions rose, political situations grew more complex, and savanna hominids, with their stone tools, became ever more reliant on preserving their cultural-based traditions. Hominids would also have benefited from a bigger brain for understanding and outwitting predators in a clever, coordinated manner. Being neither large nor fierce, we had to rely on our wits, our numbers, and our social coordination. With our new energy-rich diet, we could afford, calorie-wise, the larger brains we so desperately needed. While chimpanzees and hominid frugivores would have had to eat fruit twenty-four hours a day to support larger brains, meat eating hominids could easily pay the caloric price.

But a roadblock stood on the path to large brains: at birth, larger heads simply would not fit through the small pelvic openings that had evolved for chimpanzee-sized brains. It wasn't in the cards to significantly increase the size of the opening—that would have required a major evolutionary restructuring taking millions of years. As the last trees disappeared, our ancestors didn't have millions of years. They needed larger brains and they needed them fast!

Fortunately there was a simple solution to this quandary: allow the brain to keep growing after birth. A relatively straightforward change in a few developmental-timing genes did the trick, although it also extended the period of infant helplessness after birth. The newborn babies were no longer able to cling to their mothers as they climbed trees. Ah, but this constraint had vanished along with the trees! Nothing remained to climb. Consequently, our ancestors' brain size took a giant leap upward, the newborns becoming, literally, babes in their mothers' arms as we took up life on the savanna. Steven Stanley developed this theme in his book *Children of the Ice Age*, calling it the "terrestrial imperative." His terrestrial imperative explains why, after a lull of a few million years, large brains and stone tools suddenly appeared together shortly after the start of the ice ages.

Cut and run

Our ancestors rapidly adopted the savanna way of life. The large game kills that they scavenged had tough hides; these weren't carcasses you could just tear apart with chimpanzee hands and teeth. To surmount this difficulty, our hominid ancestors drew on an occasionally used chimpanzee cultural tradition: the manufacture and use of tools to secure food that was otherwise difficult or impossible to obtain. To this day, various tribes of jungle chimpanzees use specially trimmed twigs to extract termites from their nests, properly shaped rocks to crush nuts, and so forth. Our ancestors, in their moment of need, simply amplified this venerable trait and, as before, passed specific tool-making and tool-using traditions from one generation to the next by way of cultural imitation.

It might be hard to believe that simple broken stones can cut through tough hides, even thick elephant hides, but this is indeed the case, as Kathy Schick and Nicholas Toth have amply demonstrated. In *Making Silent Stones Speak,* they describe their "experimental anthropology." They went to Africa and did themselves what our ancestors had done—cut through tough hides with pieces of broken stone, dismembering large carcasses and carrying them off in manageable pieces before other carnivores arrived. This was, presumably, the original meaning of the phrase "cut and run."

Microscopic analysis of the earliest stone tools, and the bones associated with them, reveals scratch marks on the tools consistent with their use for cutting meat, as well as corresponding cut marks on the bones of dismembered animals. Even more illuminating is the fact that many of their bones also have carnivore tooth marks overlaid by the scratches from stone tools. Carnivores had made the kill; we were the scavengers. The largest number of bones found with early stone tools were those of antelope, part of Vrba's new suite of species that appeared on the savanna about the same time we did. They ate the grass; the lions ate them; we ate the left-over scraps..

Crossing the cultural Rubicon

Our ancestors went beyond relying on meat eating and simple tool use as occasional, supplemental behaviors. These cultural adaptations quickly became the essence of our line's survival strategy on the open savanna, our customary way of obtaining food. This shift from occasional to regular tool use set us on an altogether new path, one that clearly shows up in the fossil and artifactual records. Our oral hardware did not follow the route of the increasingly massive grinding machines of our *robustus* cousins; our ancestors' scaled-down teeth and jaws were adapting to a meat diet. Our bodies stayed smaller, more mobile—*Homo* was both a long-distance walker and a runner.

Sparse hair (except on the tops of heads) and profuse sweating allowed us to travel long distances every day even in the noonday heat of the shade-less savanna. Our simple tools, really just broken stones, began to show up in great numbers, often concentrated at what were probably camping or butchering sites some distance from the places such stones naturally occurred.

In making culturally-based tool manufacture and use an integral part of their lives, our ancestors crossed the divide from a predominantly genetic to what would eventually become a predominantly cultural world. The cultural transmission of extra-genetic information between generations became the key to their survival. A new evolutionary force on this planet had been released.

Our ancestors' primitive culture—an important aspect of their ability to make and use tools successfully in carnivore niches—emerged as a selective force in genetic evolution. Individuals with a greater capacity for the cultural transmission and retention of information, as well as those with more dexterous hands, had a slight evolutionary advantage. Their offspring were preferentially selected to continue the hominid line. The era of genetic and cultural co-evolution had arrived. A spiral of increasing intelligence, dexterity, and, eventually, sophisticated technology was the outcome.

Our early hominid tools, sometimes called the Oldowan industry, were nothing but broken or flaked stones. These simple tools, adopted some 2.5 million years ago, stayed essentially the same for almost a million years, with no noticeable improvements. Scottish-American anthropologist William McGrew, comparing chimpanzee tools used to secure food with those of the Tasmanian aborigines, concluded that the level of sophistication was similar.

Stone tools, however, may not have been nearly as important in the emergence of *Homo* as was our transition to the open savanna. Anthropologists increasingly believe that the changes our ancestors made in social organization to adapt to their new way of life may have been more important in sustaining the evolutionary spiral that produced the remarkably rapid growth of our brain. The savanna freed our brain to continue this rapid growth after birth, while challenging us to survive in large cooperative groups in competition with lions and hyenas.

In a mere million years, hominid brains exploded from a normal chimpanzee size of about 450 cubic centimeters, about the volume of an apple, to a full grapefruit of 800 cubic centimeters—nearly doubling in size. This is an extraordinarily rapid pace for genetic evolution, especially when one considers the metabolic expense of brains.

But bigger brains came in handy. Survival on the savanna required large, cooperative groups, a division of labor, and extensive sharing, especially since pregnant females or those carrying babies did not make good scavengers or hunters. Scavenging and hunting required male cooperation, penalizing excessive intragender competition. Males and females became more nearly equal in size. As brains grew and the period of postnatal helplessness lengthened, females increasingly preferred and selected helpful males who stayed with them. Honey-do's are an ancient and venerable tradition! Eventually the advantages of an ever-larger brain were offset by its increased metabolic cost and by the longer period of infant dependency. At this point, the sudden spurt of brain growth fell off. *Homo erectus* had arrived.

Encouraged by modest home-front success, *Homo erectus*, an advanced form of *Homo habilis*, spilled out of Africa into the southern regions of Asia, venturing as far east as present-day Beijing. The *erectus* who left Africa for the east took the original, rather primitive Oldowan tools with them. Amazingly, a secluded pocket of *erectus* that settled in Borneo survived until less than fifty thousand years ago. *Homo erectus* lasted longer than any other hominid species—almost two million years.

Meanwhile, back in east Africa, *erectus* developed advanced Acheulean stone tools. Far beyond broken rocks and sharp chips, Acheulean tools included carefully shaped hand axes. As before, however, once the new tools appeared, they didn't noticeably change again for a million years.

In addition to using tools, at some point—no one knows exactly when—*Homo erectus* also learned to use fire. Fire, in its various manifestations, was to change the planet, transforming ecosystems and releasing vast quantities of energy in the hands of this highly cultural line of hominids.

Humaneese—we hear what we say

Homo erectus may also have been responsible for the initiation and the early development of that other uniquely human capability, complex language. Although the experts remain divided on this question; some suggest that a proto-language evolved as early as 2.5 million years ago, while others insist that it may have been invented as recently as 40 thousand years ago.

Many different animals, especially social animals, communicate with each other. Ants, as discussed earlier, are compulsive chemical communicators; their colonies of millions are built on the cooperation inherent in their common genetic behavioral programs and, critically, on their dozen or so chemical words. Also, we have seen that chimpanzees and bonobos (such as Kanzi) can learn the meaning of a hundred or so symbols, creatively using two or three of them together to create very simple statements similar to those of a two-year-old human child. In the entire animal kingdom, however, nothing approaches the infinite generative capacity of human language.

Nor is spoken language the only means of communication between individual humans. We often use gestures, an almost automatic supplement to speaking; it is difficult to talk without gesturing. Communication also takes place when one person demonstrates to another how to perform a task. Tool making has always been a special category of communication between individuals and generations of *Homos*. Since we left the safety of the trees and took up life on the savannahs, our lives have depended on tools and on retaining the continuity of our tool-making knowledge between generations.

Language supports the ability to plan ahead, to think about and discuss things "off-line" before they actually happen, to coordinate actions, and to analyze and discuss what happened after the fact—the better to do it next time. Perhaps these traits were the key reasons why larger brains became so advantageous. The evolutionary pressure for development of language and planning must have been immense.

Creating a larger but structurally similar brain, as *Homo erectus* apparently did, turns out not to be too difficult genetically. A change in just a few developmental timing genes can cause the brain to grow for a longer duration than the rest of the body. Changing the structure of the brain is much trickier, however. Those areas of our brain that are structurally different from the chimpanzees' are primarily related to the generation and understanding of speech, or with planning and other complex mental tasks.

As our brain specialized to accommodate speech, our larynx was evolutionarily relocated and redesigned relative to that of chimpanzees. In the early evolution of land animals, food and air passages crossed. The larynx evolved in terrestrial vertebrates so that animals wouldn't choke on their food while breathing. For them it works well; animals can actually eat and breathe at the same time—all animals, that is, except us. Our larynx was reconfigured to accommodate speech, to rapidly produce a wide range of sounds. However, this rather slipshod redesign allow food to enter our windpipe if we breathed while eating. Evolutionary selection pressures for improved speech simply carried much more weight than did the penalties of a few deaths from food directed down the wrong pipe.

Once language—even simple language—got off the ground, there was bound to be considerable selection pressure to mate with those who spoke (or gestured) better and were therefore more socially adept. Improved vocal skills would have offered other selective advantages, such as increased political power, effective courtship, and better care of children.

Many rapid changes in animals were due to out-of-control arms races between two different species, such as the speed of a predator and its primary prey. For our ancestors, the intelligence arms race may have been a within-species, family affair. Modern humans, as a result, are fast talkers—we can produce distinct sound segments at the amazingly rapid rate of up to twenty-five per second.

Potato diggers bite the dust

While *Homo erectus* was making its debut and evolving onward, what was happening to the other eastern apes? What was the gorilla-like *robustus* up to? *Robustus,* in fact, was also getting smarter, but unfortunately their advancement was too little, too late, and they finally went extinct about one million years ago. Presumably, *robustus* lost out in the survival competition with our much smarter, chattier ancestors. *Robustus* might also have gotten the evolutionary squeeze from the fast-rising and increasingly successful baboons, who invaded their ecological niche of digging up underground vegetables.

Perhaps in the long run there may have been ecological room on our planet for only one species with the capacity for culture. The first species to acquire significant culture would eventually eliminate any cultural competitors, nipping any such newly appearing species in the bud.

Roll the drums—*Homo sapiens*

About 900 thousand years ago, after a million years of relative stasis with *Homo erectus*, our lineage finally unveiled a new physique and tool kit, as the second onslaught of the Ice Age struck the Earth. The most famous (but not the most typical) of these archaic homo sapiens were the Neanderthals. Based on large stone flakes, the latest hominid toolkit contained more than sixty kinds of implements. As before, the latest model was produced in Africa and eventually headed north and east, this time directly into the teeth of the deepening Ice Age.

Living in Europe through the second half of the last Ice Age, Neanderthals were, despite their cave-man reputation, highly advanced. Their specialized culture allowed them to thrive in an extremely cold climate. Neanderthals had a brain as large as ours, perhaps slightly larger. Neanderthals most likely had at least a gestural language, although their spoken language may have been rudimentary.

Finally, sometime less than 200 thousand years ago, biologically modern *Homo sapiens* made their African debut. Improved tools followed this new hominid model after the usual lag time; its—excuse me, *our*—new toolkit featured narrow-blade instead of wide-blade technology. Instead of sixty types of implements, we had well over a hundred. Several African sites show the new, considerably advanced tools appearing by ninety thousand years ago. The physical and mental makeup of our ancestors was probably identical to our own today. Properly dressed and shorn, any *Homo sapiens* from 100 thousand years ago wouldn't raise an eyebrow today in a cosmopolitan area. They were thoroughly modern; any one of them could have learned to fly a 747, although mastering a child-proof safety cap would have baffled them as much as it does us. With them, we essentially reached the present human genetic condition.

Most all the significant changes since then have been cultural, not genetic. One can grasp the recent origin of modern humanity and our genetic similarity to each other when one realizes that genetic diversity among humans is only one-fiftieth of the genetic diversity among chimpanzees. It's true—human racial differences are completely insignificant.

A planetary sweep

Soon after its debut in Africa, the latest human model headed out from the homeland. Reaching the Middle East, always the crossroads of the world, some *sapiens* pressed onward into Asia, while others headed west into Europe, still in the grip of an ice age. Sixty thousand years ago, they reached Australia. From fifty thousand years ago in Eastern Europe to thirty thousand years ago in Western Europe, the *sapiens* invaders systematically replaced the Neanderthals. Twenty thousand years after their cohabitation began, the Neanderthals were gone. Results were similar whenever modern humans encountered *Archaic sapiens*: the latter simply disappeared. We don't know the reason. Perhaps Neanderthals and other *Archaic sapiens* lacked a fully modern spoken language, relying primarily on more primitive gestures for communication. If so, our ancestors may have attacked them at night when the spoken word could coordinate the aggressors but the gestural word's nighttime inefficacy left the victims helpless. For whatever reason, none of the Neanderthals survived.

By twenty thousand years ago, equipped with finely tailored parkas and other cold-weather gear, *sapiens* invaded arctic Siberia and, shortly thereafter, hiked and hunted their way across the Bering Strait land bridge to Alaska. There, a vast ice sheet temporarily blocked them, but about twelve thousand years ago, a glacial corridor opened—a southern passage. In only a thousand years, the ancestors of the indigenous Americans forged a path from Alaska to the southern tip of South America. A seafaring group also left Southeast Asia to settle the South

Pacific islands, reaching Hawaii in the era of Socrates and New Zealand about the time of King Arthur and Sir Lancelot's falling out. In well under a thousand centuries, *Homo sapiens* came to occupy all the land areas on this planet except Antarctica.

Beginning about forty thousand years ago in Western Europe, tools of the very finest form appeared. Delicately struck in antler as well as in stone, these implements were often, literally, works of art. Cave painting, sculpting, and engraving were in evidence, although perhaps not yet common. Wherever *sapiens* ventured, we find similar displays of the modern mind at work. The era of long-lasting static toolkits had come to an end after a two-million year hegemony. From this point on, continuous change was to be the norm.

Quite some time ago, we invented the spear and, not long after that, the bow and arrow. These weapons allowed our ancestors to kill large game with relative impunity, since the normally lethal but close range defenses of large animals could not be brought to bear on such well-equipped human hunters. In Africa, Europe, and to some extent Asia, animals had become acclimated to earlier human hunters, *Archaic sapiens*. The beasts had learned, over many generations, to avoid this dangerous top predator. The large mammals of Africa certainly had an early start in treating primate bipeds with suspicion, witnessing every increment of our technological advance. But when large animals that had never encountered a hominid suddenly met spear-equipped humans, the results were predictably and uniformly disastrous for the animals. Australia and the Americas were, to put it mildly, a turkey shoot for our ancestors. Three-quarters of the large mammalian species died out on both continents, presumably driven to total extinction by human hunting. Our kind—prior to any civilization—seems to have caused the greatest extinction of large animals since an asteroid wiped out the dinosaurs some 65 million years ago.

And this sweep was only the beginning. Ten thousand years ago we had arrived at a major turning point in our evolutionary history. In our hands now lay the power to transform human culture and the very planet with blinding speed.

Chapter 6

CIVILIZATIONS
The chimpanzees who became ants

It may be argued that the animal within us is our noble side,
and humanity or civilization the blacker side—
a complete reversal of the Victorian image.
Samuel Butler

Generations have trod, have trod, have trod;
And all is seared with trade; bleared, smeared with toil;
And wears man's smudge and share's man's smell:
The soil is bare now, nor can foot feel, being shod.
Gerard Manley Hopkins

An unlikely candidate

As planet-wide top predators at the end of the Ice Age, our species seemed an unlikely candidate to break through to the superorganism level pioneered by the ants and other social insects. Individualists, we lacked the selfless, unquestioning communist instincts of the social insects that brought them superorganism success through the smooth cooperation of thousands, even millions of sisters. Furthermore, *Homo sapiens* came in only two varieties: male and female. We had no inborn caste structure and thus little inherent specialization. Everyone was a generalist.

Our tendency to live in small bands was another roadblock on the path to large-scale organization. We moved on as we exhausted local concentrations of food or our accumulated filth rendered a location unpleasant or unhealthy. Our largest groupings naturally and inevitably split apart if they became too big for everyone to nose into everyone else's business—when their numbers grew too great for personal interactions on a daily basis. Massed, insect-like togetherness didn't seem to be our forte.

Worst of all, we ate at the wrong end of the food chain—the top instead of the bottom. We were rare, as top predators and omnivores must always be. Our biomass was minuscule; less than five million of us existed planet-wide during our hunter-gatherer heyday. One would be hard-pressed to find an animal less suited to a future as a populous, biomass superstar!

Ecologically, we faced the same sort of situation as the primitive hunter-gatherer ants had before they discovered herding and farming. Like them, we lacked the internal cellulose-digesting bacteria of cows or termites. The only way we could become numerous was by mimicking the ants who had tapped the bottom of the food chain via sophisticated control of other species. As we have seen, some of these ants let other species (aphids) digest plants for them. Other ants grew their own digestible food (fungi) in gardens. Only if we emulated herding ants, farming ants, or both, could we grab a more generous portion of the planetary pie. But why would *Homo sapiens* want to do such a thing?

The savage myth

It's a popular misconception that prior to agriculture and civilization we had to work hard all day long just to get enough to eat, that we were always hanging on the edge of starvation—much too busy hunting and gathering to have any free time. At night, this fable continues, our ancestors retreated to the protection of caves. Large fires in the cave's entrances held vicious animals at bay, their hungry eyes reflecting our firelight. One day, it is supposed, some green-thumbed Einstein discovered the result of planting seeds. Almost overnight, agriculture gave humans abundant food with little work, granting us the leisure time to form civilizations. As the surrounding hunter-gatherers realized the overwhelming benefits of agriculture and civilization, they jumped on the agricultural bandwagon. And that, to conclude the story, is how we civilized nearly the entire planet in only a few thousand years. The problem is, this story is totally wrong!

Social anthropologists, who have studied the few remaining hunter-gatherer societies, paint a starkly different picture. They point out that hunter-gatherers work only a few hours a day (if their varied and healthful activities can even be called work). In this short time they secure a balanced and nutritious diet high in protein and fiber and low in fat and carbohydrates. They have no incentive to work more than this and rarely do. This leaves them with what seems to us like an inordinate amount of leisure time, which they devote to gossiping, telling stories, participating in social activities, and just relaxing—not to mention the occasional excitement of intertribal warfare.

Physical anthropologists, for their part, have assessed humanity's health prior to and after the advent of agriculture and civilization. Based on skeletal remains, they have concluded that our ancestors were well fed before agriculture, but poorly fed afterwards. A diet of mainly "cheap" grain carbohydrates isn't particularly healthy.

Finally, to rebut the core of the erroneous fable, it seems likely that hunter-gatherers have always been quite aware of the life cycles of the plants and animals around them. No dolts, they knew what seeds and sex produced. Thus, the popular notion of stone-age humanity's conversion to an agricultural way of life, falls wide of the mark. We should also note that since the dawn of civilization, mobile hunter-gatherers have had many chances to voluntarily take up agriculture and its sedentary ways, but have repeatedly rejected such "opportunities." Hunter-gatherers aren't dummies; they know it takes more work to produce food by herding or farming than it does by hunting and gathering. To eke out a living, farmers must toil much harder and longer than hunter-gatherers. Instead of just picking and eating the end result, farmers must also clear the land, plant seeds, and keep weeds and other would-be consumers, both human and non-human, at bay. Worst of all, this hard, repetitious labor takes place in open fields under the hot sun. Only slavery, force of arms, or the threat of starvation have forced indigenous people to succumb to the pains of agricultural life.

The hunter-gatherer lifestyle remained well suited to humanity as long as population density stayed low and game and other food abounded. Their naturally high-protein, low-carbohydrate diet and frequent exercise kept their body fat low, resulting in low female fertility (which increases with body fat).

Breast-feeding each child for four years or more also served to decrease fertility, since nursing suppresses ovulation. Nor were mothers, who walked a couple of thousand miles every year, thrilled with the thought of multiple babes-in-arms, another result of the terrestrial imperative we met in the last chapter.

Our hunting and gathering lifestyle evolved over a couple of million years and proved healthy, both physically and mentally. Evolution adapted us to be hunter-gatherers, so why didn't we just stay happy and healthy as we were? The answer, in short, is that we became the unwitting victims of our own success. It is a common evolutionary story. As we shall see, our success blocked the road back to our Garden of Eden. We could only go onward and upward or crash to extinction.

We become farmers

As mentioned in the previous chapter, cultural information began to snowball about fifty thousand years ago. A rapid improvement in hunting technology led to our increased reliance on meat from large mammals, as even the biggest, meanest animals couldn't match our spears and coordinated hunting parties. Our population inevitably rose. The problem, however, was that we killed off large game much faster than it replaced itself. Thus, the game on which we had come to depend began its steep decline. For many game species, this decline led to their extinction. To make matters worse, we could no longer emigrate to unoccupied, game-rich territory. Our cultural knowledge as a species had, by way of boats and cold-weather parkas, already allowed us to populate the entire planet except Antarctica.

The archaeological record shows a clear shift from large to small game as the Ice Age drew to a close some twelve thousand years ago. This change occurred slightly later in the New World, as we had occupied it more recently. Hunters secured less meat per hour of effort with small game than with large, but they had little choice. As small game and wild fruits and vegetables became scarce, we shifted to slash-and-burn agriculture and to pastoral herding. Finally, as good land for these methods became scarce, portions of humanity turned, as a last resort, to sedentary agriculture. Given the options of starving to death or staying in one place and farming, we chose to farm. It was as simple as that. Our hunting success sealed our fate; we had no other option.

Within the space of a few thousand years, widely separated groups around the planet turned to agriculture. This closeness in timing was probably not due to the diffusion of basic agricultural knowledge, which was already widespread, but to population pressure. It may also have been due to the arrival of mild weather that was conducive to agriculture. When our combined population threatened to exceed what the planet could support as hunter-gatherers or slash-and-burn agriculturalists, sedentary farming gave us the means for not only for continued survival, but even for growth.

Our two-part agricultural strategy

Farming, as our ancestors developed it, had a two-part, plant-animal strategy. First, we made common those usually rare plants—the grains, vegetables, and fruits we omnivores could eat directly. Out of the millions of plant species on Earth, humans have considered only a couple of hundred worth cultivating. At the same time, we actively discouraged inedible plants from growing and reproducing, causing them to be much less plentiful than they naturally would have been. We physically altered the landscape, clearing, leveling, and plowing it to benefit our chosen species. Directly planting the seeds of our favored few, we relentlessly attacked any other life, plant or animal, that dared to encroach on our humanly-created ecosystems.

The second, animal part of our agricultural strategy was to make common those animals we found useful while rendering competing animals rare. But why did we bother with animals at all? On the savannahs, as small bands of hominids, it will be remembered, meat was our ticket to *sapiens* status. But as agriculturists, our plentiful crops were our ticket to reproductive success. Wouldn't we have been better off just eating plants at the bottom of the food chain? Why pass precious food through other animals first, thereby losing much of its energy? Why eat anything at all off the top of the food chain?

Vegetarians are living proof that humans can survive while eating only plants (although fruits and nuts are, in a sense, also at the top of the food chain). But survival is one thing; obtaining a nutritious balance of proteins is quite another. Vegetarians struggle to achieve such a balance. This is not surprising since our species has, over several million years, adapted to eating significant amounts of meat. Because meat is a naturally balanced source of protein, we have, over time, lost the ability to create several essential amino acids from plant food alone. Although we can still obtain these amino acids with a careful combination of plant foods, meat and other animal products provide the same nutrition in a more efficient, convenient, and tasty manner.

Not only was meat our best source of protein, it even came as something of an agricultural freebie, since cattle, goats, and sheep can exist on plant food that we ourselves can't use directly, such as the straw and stubble left over from harvesting grains. Furthermore, many parcels of land are ill-suited for farming but are appropriate for grazing. Also, since we can eat only certain favored parts of many vegetables; why waste the unused portions? Better to feed them to domesticated animals, thereby providing ourselves with a source of balanced protein by way of their meat, milk, or blood. In addition, domesticated animals don't just produce valuable protein; they also provide a source of fiber for clothes, hides for shoes and tents, and fertilizer for gardens. Some of these animals, especially cattle, supplied useful power for pulling plows and transporting material on sledges or, later, on wheeled carts.

Together, humans and our domesticated plants and animals formed an efficient team. Together, we have rapidly taken over the planet, achieving combined biomass dominance through our cooperative effort. No one can deny the biological effectiveness of our cooperative agricultural strategy—right up there with the herding and gardening ants.

With agriculture, we took charge of evolution. Just as we'd known about seeds and life cycles since time immemorial, so too we had known about heredity. The plants we favored for continued propagation in our ecosystems tended to be easier and faster to grow and cultivate, to be more convenient to process and store, and to have larger edible portions that were tastier, more nutritious, and less toxic. We preferred animal offspring that were less agile and more passive, that had furrier coats, or that could pull larger plows.

Domesticates are not so much wild species held against their will as they are new species that thrive alongside humans in our unique self-made environment. Domesticates are our partners in a brave new world order. Their wild relatives have faded or been driven to extinction. The "kept" plant or animal's life may not be as free and exciting as life in the wild but, from an evolutionary point of view, domestication elevated a few chosen species to planetary stardom.

Various species of ants have practiced sedentary agriculture for well over twenty million years. Humans, however, were the first mammals to engage in such agriculture and, of course, the first species of any sort to combine a sizable number of different plant and animal domesticates in the creation of new ecosystems. Three major consequences resulted from this biologically unique development: a booming population, unhealthy lifestyles, and a modest food surplus that launched civilization.

Ag 1—Booming population

The first consequence was that once an area became agricultural, its population—human and domesticate—boomed. Compared to natural ecosystems harvested by hunter-gatherers, intensive agriculture can easily support a *thousand* times as many people on the same area of land. Sedentary mothers no longer needed to carry their children about, so the birth rate rose. Furthermore, agriculture generally produces a high-carbohydrate, low-protein diet that naturally leads to body fat and hence to increased female fertility. Baby boom!

As human and domesticate numbers soared, local populations of game and edible wild fruit and tubers plummeted; there is, after all, only so much space, water, and sunshine to go around. The street from hunter-gatherer to sedentary agriculturist was one-way. Agriculture and its attendant population growth was the can't–go–back ratchet that propelled humanity, like it or not, toward planetary dominance. The logical outcome, unless we become the first species in four billion years to voluntarily restrain its success, will be that we will turn all the natural ecosystems on the planet into one gigantic human agricultural ecosystem—or go bust trying to make it happen.

Ag 2—Unhealthy lifestyle

The second consequence of settled agriculture was a turn for the worse in the lifestyles and health of the great masses of individual humans. Food was no longer an inalienable right, free to all for the picking or hunting. Obtaining sustenance required long hours of hard, monotonous work in the hot sun. The fruits of our labor were less varied and less nutritious. Grains are concentrated energy sources that can be grown relatively easily and store well. Nature, after all, evolved them to be hardy seeds. Although grains are calorie-rich, they are low in protein and lack a number of essential amino acids and nutrients. The malnutrition of early farmers is evident in their skeletal remains; physical anthropologists have conclusively established that rickets spread throughout the population. Humans shortened noticeably, losing several inches in height—inches we didn't regain until modern times provided a more varied diet.

Stunted farmers didn't suffer only from malnutrition. By living continuously in one place, they accumulated food and filth that attracted pests and parasites. Many new diseases developed from our cohabitation with farm animals, our domesticated partners. Our failure to frequently pick up and move to new locations led to continuous re-infections. Again, skeletal remains make it clear that, in contrast to the healthy hunter-gatherers, diseases constantly plagued agricultural societies.

Sedentary life also had undesirable psychological effects. In cases of serious disputes, people were no longer free to pick up and move elsewhere—there were no easy outs. And, as population density skyrocketed, the number of individuals with whom one had to interact soon rose beyond the modest number we had evolved to handle comfortably. We frequently found ourselves forced to deal with strangers.

Unlike ants, that had millions of years to genetically adjust themselves to mass togetherness, we achieved our astounding agricultural success almost overnight. Only one step removed from easy-going, fruit-eating jungle chimpanzees, we were (and are) evolutionarily suited at heart to a hunter-gatherer lifestyle; agricultural toil goes against our nature.

Ag 3—Modest surpluses launch civilization

The third and final consequence of sedentary agriculture was the generation of a modest food surplus. Hunter-gatherers don't work any more than necessary to obtain their daily food; there's no reason for them to do so. Their mobility means they can't take extra food with them (or much else for that matter). But non-mobile farmers, this new breed, could save up food for a rainy day or trade food for other goods. This gave them an incentive to work for more than just their personal daily food—under the right circumstances, they might be enticed to generate a surplus.

Since agriculture is much less labor efficient than hunting and gathering, it could easily have turned out that farmers would barely have been able to grow enough food to feed themselves, leaving no surplus at all for others. Conversely, it's conceivable that, though we had to stay put and work harder, the surpluses might have been truly sizable, ushering in a golden age for all. As it happened, the results of farming (prior to machines) was that, on the average, nine hard-working farming families living near the edge of subsistence could generate just enough surplus to support one non-agricultural family.

This very slight surplus, small as it was, was our species' ticket to superorganism status, to cities of thousands and then millions, and to an accumulation of information the likes of which the planet had never seen. As the golden age of hunting and gathering faded from our memories, humanity set its shoulder to the plow to generate the modest surplus of food it laid aside for the future or for purchasing pottery, tools, or irresistible trinkets made by an emerging group of specialized craftsmen who gathered together in centrally located villages.

With no need to pack up and move on, the accumulation of such goods became fashionable. The consumer society emerged, thousands of years ago, at the farm and village levels.

The origins of civilizations

Villages quickly became the seats of local governments. At first, village chiefs provided a redistribution service that benefited all concerned. Their representatives collected surpluses from successful farmers, dispensing village-manufactured goods in return. The chiefs transferred goods from those with more to those with less, and provided for the common good by storing food for lean times or village celebrations. In addition, chiefs organized the common defense of the village and its associated farms.

This initially equitable arrangement between the villagers and the farmers openly invited exploitation. It is a simple fact that surpluses have always attract clever exploiters—this is biological evolution's M.O. We shouldn't be surprised, should in fact expect, that as surplus food accumulated in centralized villages, some clever humans would latch onto it in a less-than-equitable manner.

Perhaps the top-down control by the chiefs was initially benign, but crafty minds soon saw the golden opportunities surplus production created. Increased top-level control was soon applied. It led to more work for the masses and to larger surpluses for the few. Once this runaway positive-feedback process began, it continued until it generated the maximum possible control (and hence the greatest possible surpluses) for the leaders. As the fist of government control tightened, transfers increasingly ran from the poor to the already wealthy. As American anthropologist George Cowgill put it, "A degree of exploitation considered criminal by one generation was tolerated by the next and was soon hallowed by elite-inspired ideology as built into the structure of the cosmos."

This, then, is how easy-going, egalitarian, chimpanzee-like humans were transformed into industrious, hard-working, ant-like cogs in civilized superorganisms. Although we lacked the self-sacrificing spirit of ants, near total top-down control brought out the human animal's full potential—such as it was—to produce surplus food. A few humans at the top could convince (or force) the bulk of the other humans to work from sunup to sundown doing repetitious but productive labor while consuming a diet of cheaply produced grain. The ticket to human happiness and health was, of course, to be among the elite in charge, and stay in charge down through the generations. The first systems that evolved to achieve such all-encompassing control were the human superorganisms we call city-states. Reminiscent of colonies of ants, these regimented entities captured humanity.

Politicians—the more things change...

It's tempting to think that the elite seized control by the direct, crude force of arms. All governments, however, even the most despotic, primarily rely on voluntary obedience. It is considerably more efficient to have willing, cooperative, and occasionally even enthusiastic subjects, than to try to govern those who feel oppressed, coerced, or unfairly treated. So how did the leaders of early civilizations convince the farming masses to not only bust their chops working hard all day, but to permanently contribute a generous portion of their hard-won surpluses to the city elite?

First, leaders provided real services. The most important of these was the protection by a full-time army against the armies of other city-states. Nothing ruins a farmer's day faster than being captured or having an attacking horde trample his fields and burn down his house. Another vital service was the production and distribution of farm implements, such as plows and pottery. And public works—especially the development and maintenance of irrigation systems—clearly benefited everyone. Trade with distant city-states expanded the scope of available materials and products. Finally, the maintenance of law and order was an invaluable, albeit much abused, service. Instead of the comfort of small face-to-face tribes and bands, we now depended on total strangers for protection and for many of life's essentials. The state introduced new conventions—values, rituals, and laws—to replace the lost, small group, I've-known-you-all-your-life social glue. These have been termed "cultural workarounds" by cultural evolutionary theorists Peter Richerson and Robert Boyd. Such cultural workarounds allow us to function in large groups in spite of our genetic endowment that would, normally, only allow the functioning of small groups.

Besides offering actual services, elites—especially their leaders—provided legitimacy through clever, self-serving claims of supposed service. This included the claim that inequality was not only necessary, but was in the public interest. *The Epic of Gilgamesh,* humanity's most ancient written story, contains political exhortations by Gilgamesh, an early Sumerian king. The similarities of his proclamations to the speeches of current politicians are amazing. They covered, among other things, protection of the weak from the strong and assistance for the blind and aged. Human psychology hasn't changed significantly since the dawn of civilization. People want to believe. They want to hear the words spoken, even if the vision falls pathetically short of reality. Politicians have routinely offered the masses soothing messages while bleeding them dry.

The origin of state religions

Even prior to civilizations, astute leaders understood the human tendency to surrender power to another "higher" person—seeking the warm comfort of dependency. State rulers, no less astute than their predecessors, did their best to convince their subjects that they were wise and benevolent yet powerful father figures, and that the state—although really distant and faceless—was a close and warm extended family. The rulers surrounded themselves with symbols of family, power, and authority. They encouraged hero worship. They drew on kinship terms and practices to simulate the family relationship. And they united the masses under the banner of religion.

Humans yearn for the assurance that physical death is not final, that we belong to something larger than ourselves, that somehow life all makes sense and will, in the end, turn out to be fair, just, and glorious. Some scholars claim that early state-sponsored religions were just façades the elite used to intimidate their subjects and legitimize their privileged access to scarce resources. This view certainly holds some truth. But religions also provided a genuine service. One suspects that priests and other practitioners were, for the most part, true believers, not charlatans. While it may be true, as Karl Marx cynically suggested, that religion is the convenient, state-sponsored "opiate of the masses," it is also true that with the stress brought on by agriculture and civilization, the formerly easy-going hunter-gatherers badly needed an opiate. As civilization increased life's complexities, conflicts, and hardships, we desperately desired to make sense of it all and to be comforted.

Always in the background, prompting our subconscious minds, hung the threat of coercion. The knowledge that the state was the source of one's food and one's very existence, that the state had the power to punish, even kill those who opposed it, and that there was nowhere else to go (especially for civilizations surrounded by barren deserts or hostile neighbors) tended to entice the state's subjects to voluntarily follow the rules. When all else failed, however, leaders could turn to the direct use of force, which few states have ever hesitated to apply as a last resort.

Early city-states—human ant colonies

The first expressions of the planet's newest superorganisms were the city-states in Sumer on the flat plains of Mesopotamia, where the intensive agriculture of these city-states took advantage of the nearly level land. For over two hundred miles, the Tigris and Euphrates rivers fall only about one hundred feet in elevation, approximately half a foot per mile. This level land, already mostly devoid of trees, was quite desert-like, yet the rivers provided copious quantities of water. The catch was that irrigation channels had to be dug and maintained, and this required a high degree of planning and central control.

Irrigation produced bountiful yields of grain and other food. Although its food yield per hour of direct labor was relatively higher than earlier agriculture's, it took more labor to keep the irrigation systems in order and more administrators to manage these complex societies; greater yield but higher overhead.

Castrating domestic cattle gave us oxen—docile animals that could pull large plows across the level fields with ease. Oxen and plows, when combined with fallowing, promised seemingly perpetual use of the same fields. Fallowing is a neat trick. Farmers allow all the non-domesticated plants to germinate and grow. Then, before the unwanted plants—weeds—have a chance to go to seed, they plow them all under, not only killing off the competition to the domesticated plants, but also providing them with important nutrients in the process.

The combination of tightly-controlled human labor, irrigation, and oxen-pulled plows yielded large surpluses. This highly organized approach to agriculture proved an efficient way, in a small, controllable area, of producing amounts of food significantly beyond what farmers needed for bare subsistence. The result: real cities, not just villages. Now the non-food-producing elites could cluster behind protective walls. Large, permanent cities began to dot the plains of Mesopotamia like so many anthills, joining the ant colonies, beehives, and termite nests as the planet's most complex communities. At least in Mesopotamia, we humans had moved a major step up the evolutionary ladder of hierarchical complexity. We had, in only a few thousand years accomplished the move from a mere social species to true superorganism status, the move it had taken the ants millions of years to achieve. Way to go humanity!

Bigger armies are better

The immediate challenge of these city-states, these human superorganisms, was survival. As with ant colonies, the stiffest competition, the greatest threat, came from similar superorganisms. Like our insect counterparts, larger human colonies had a decisive competitive edge, for they could support a more numerous caste of full-time soldiers. This basic biological fact about superorganisms did not escape the notice of those in charge of the earliest city-states. Their primary goal, in a nutshell, was to control the greatest number of peasants possible. In that way, they could produce the largest surpluses and hence field the largest armies to protect their city-states and, while they were at it, raid smaller, weaker neighboring states.

The degree of central control fell off rapidly with distance, however. Little control was feasible beyond a day's walk. Thus, early city-states had to support as many people as they could within a limited area, producing enough surplus food to feed a sizeable army. After all, once superorganisms appeared on the scene, life was primarily about armies, about superorganism survival. Gone for the masses were equality, leisure time, freedom from want, and the uncrowded, wide open spaces of nature. They were replaced with regimentation, poverty, grinding toil, disease and, for many, slavery. For ants, hard work, military organization, and even slavery were old hat. Ants to Sumerians: "Welcome to the world of superorganisms!"

From the biological, though probably unconscious viewpoint of those in control, it all made perfect sense. They already thought like ants: the hard work of the lower castes was of little or no direct consequence to them. But we should not necessarily tag them as being evil or selfish. They were simply trying to maintain and protect their superorganisms, to prevent their rivals from devastating their city-states. Only a superior army could save kings, priests, and farmers alike from death or capture. Ironically, the farmers who had learned how to control other species now fell subject to such control themselves. May the punishment fit the crime.

Origins of writing—the number crunchers

While it paid well, controlling a society was never easy. Many greedy hands and hungry mouths intervened between the peasants at the bottom and the leaders at the top. The Sumerian priests—the first bosses—invented a clever means of ensuring that their lackeys did indeed channel the valuable surpluses collected from the peasants to the elite, that unscrupulous underlings didn't siphon off too much bounty along the way, that upstart farmers didn't hoard their harvests to begin with—aspiring to rise above their assigned lot of bare subsistence.

Sumerian priests invented the first accounting system, a way to keep accurate track of the sheep, cows, and sacks of grain.

Accountants used marble-sized clay tokens to stand for the various heads of livestock or sacks of grain. They represented the output of a farm or a district with an appropriate number of different clay tokens, the smallest tokens standing for single units, larger tokens for ten or sixty, one type of token for sheep, another for goats, and so on. They placed these tokens in a clay jar, closed the top with fresh clay, and rolled the seal of authority across the wet lid. Stored on an appropriate shelf at the local temple, this permanent record helped keep everyone honest. If a question or quarrel arose, officials could always break open the appropriate jar and count the tokens.

As we all know, records alone do not make honest tax payers, not to mention tax collectors. Were farmers and tax collectors really toeing the line? The priests were well aware of human nature. Not only was an accounting system necessary, but soon enough it became clear that an auditing system was also required. It can be imagined that some early priest gave an especially bright, loyal collector the important job of spot-checking the system. Not long after a tax accountant tallied some farmer's production—and both had imprinted their seals on the fresh clay jar top and deposited the jar on the tax records shelf—the auditor, making a random selection, would break the jar open, count the tokens, and then in person go out to the farm in question and count the actual assets. If the auditor found any shortcomings in the tax that had been paid, the cheaters felt the full force of the punitive power of the state.

This accounting and auditing system operated smoothly, and the priests did well. It was a bit of a pain, however, to break open jars, count tokens, and then reseal them in new jars, not to mention the expense this process incurred. One day, a creative, efficiency-minded auditor suggested that before sealing the jars, the tokens could be pressed on the outer front surface of the still-fresh clay. This way, the auditor could check on the farmers and assessors by reading the front of the jar without having to break it open. Please note that the work of making the impressions, of filling out this first tax form, was incumbent on the farmer, not on the tax collector, and certainly not on the priest's auditor!

Within a few generations, the temple librarian, perhaps a great grandson of the creative young auditor, faced a growing shortage of shelf space for tax jars. In another stroke of efficiency-inspired genius, he suggested that they dispense with tokens and jars altogether. The curved jar fronts contained the same information as the tokens within the jar, and jar fronts alone would take up less space since they could be neatly stacked. Thus, the first clay tablets had arrived, complete with curved fronts and token impressions. They were the first IRS Form 1040s.

Only a few short steps remained to replace token imprints with stylus marks, flatten out the jar fronts, and add symbols for non-accounting information, such as ideas and even spoken sounds. Writing had arrived! The Sumerians eventually employed more than one thousand different symbols in their cuneiform writing system.

The Sumerian's complex writing system was difficult to master, so the first schools were established some five thousand years ago. The earliest preserved writing, according to one archeologist, comes from student exercises at the school on #1 Broad Street in Uruk. Most specialists in those days learned their occupations through on-the-job training, usually from their parents, but training scribes required the formality of schools and professional teachers, and involved long hours of drills and dull lessons. Apparently, the more things change, the more they stay the same.

Boring or not, the combination of writing, schools, and stored copies of written material—early libraries—began an accumulation of extra-genetic information, transcending localities, generations, and even languages. This culturally-born information eventually outstripped, in pure volume, all the information our line had accumulated genetically over some four billion years. Clay tax forms and clever accountants were the spark that ignited a revolution in communication and education that led to written language, libraries, and all the great human institutions of learning, forever changing the planet. Let's hear it for the number-crunchers—the tax accountants and auditors that started it all!

Beyond superorganisms—human empires

Cities accumulated the surpluses generated by irrigation and plowing as stored grain, gold, and various other goodies for the armies, priests, and Sumerian elite. This concentrated wealth irresistibly tempted would-be looters, requiring a permanent and specialized military caste to protect both the wealth and its owners. In the competition between city-states, those that needlessly left surpluses with the farmers or squandered them on excessive temple-building eventually lost out. City-states that taxed their farmers more heavily or squandered less had bigger and better-equipped armies and, in the end, conquered the less-efficient, less-disciplined city-states. Therefore, prudent Sumerian rulers always taxed their farmers to the max and ran a tight ship, spending most of their surpluses on the military. The arms race was off and running: horses, chariots, bigger cities, and soon—in another tradition pioneered by the ants, although rather weakly—multi-city empires appeared.

Sumerian priests originally ran human superorganisms from their city temples, which sat on the pinnacles of artificially generated mountains, often the residue of earlier temples. This topophilia speaks to the human mind's instinctive tendency to equate large size and elevated physical position with awesome, god-like power. The priests discovered this psychological trick early on. But too many priests and temples diverted resources away from the military, and a weak military leads to being conquered. The inevitable corrective: military instead of religious control. With the military elite now exercising more forceful and direct control of the masses, religions began to emphasize the use of persuasion rather than force to entice the masses to work hard, while suffering their many privations with cheerful spirits. Religions could indeed work miracles!

Around the time of Gilgamesh (2700 BC), the frequency and intensity of warfare in Sumer increased dramatically. This wasn't so much due to fights over limited resources as to the ability of a few densely populated states to field large armies and to overcome smaller armies. The rewards, as in ant warfare, were territorial expansion and the capture of slaves and booty.

With Gilgamesh, King of Uruk, the first long-distance campaigning began, and the Sumerians quickly walled their cities. By 2500 BC, stone weapons were out; bronze helmets, swords, and the composite bow were in. Early horses were not yet large enough to ride, but were capable of pulling loads—hence the four-horsepower battle wagons that soon appeared. A warrior culture, separate from the rest of civilized society, originated in those times and has continued to the present day. Exclusively masculine, it cherished and rewarded confrontation and violence, in sharp contrast to the generally cooperative, non-combative outlook of civilians.

The combination of long-distance campaigning and written communications—which could be sent long distances under the King's seal—allowed a number of city-states to cooperate, minimizing between-state infighting. Sargon of Akkad ruled the first extensive human civilization. Over the course of more than thirty different wars, he forged an empire corresponding roughly to the borders of modern Iraq that lasted from 2340 to 2284 BC. His campaigns outside this empire reached as far as Lebanon and southern Turkey.

While empires could have forced entire conquered peoples into inferior classes, the dynamics of empire-building actually mitigated some of the harsher aspects of civilization. Emperors carefully cultivated their image as wise and benevolent rulers among potential subject populations, luring them into the empire with minimal fighting. "Join us, and the empire will protect you from overly zealous local tax collectors," they suggested sweetly. The emperor, trying to curry public favor, often portrayed himself as a friend of the downtrodden farming masses.

Empires never took off among ants, but with humans it was a completely different story. With empires, we can readily discern the emergence of the modern hierarchy of a humanly-dominated world order. Empires controlled vassal states. Within these states, kings ruled the mass of farmers. The farmers, in turn, managed domesticated plants and animals. Some of these domesticated animals, such as cows, contained trillions of cellulose-digesting bacteria. The bacteria ...hierarchy ad infinitum.

Unintended consequences

Not all was well, however, for there was a basic flaw to be found in humanity's unconscious strategy for planetary domination. The flaw lay in the ironic fact that the artificial ecosystems we had created to favor our own preferred species of domesticated plants and animals also happened to favor a few other species of life—the law of unintended consequences in action. Plants and animals were, in a way, competing to be "adopted" by the newly dominant humans; they were all looking for a free ride—on our coattails. The only difference between wheat and weeds, for instance, was that we had no use for weeds. Yet we have, in a sense, domesticated both wheat and weeds, as they both thrive in artificial, humanly-created ecosystems.

Even more problematic than weeds was the inadvertent domestication of such charming companions as rats and other vermin of all kinds, not to mention viruses, bacteria, and other assorted free-riders that viewed our masses of intentionally domesticated plants and animals as irresistible meals. Some of these nasty creatures eyed the high species concentrations of *Homo sapiens* (and our wastes) as a veritable feast. Although our own genetic evolution, and that of other large animals, is slow, that of fast-breeding bacteria and viruses moves rapidly indeed. Pathogens quickly took advantage of the new opportunities civilization afforded them. Civilization turned out to be a raw deal for the toiling human masses at the bottom, but it was a fabulous boon for a few well-adapted microbes and such larger parasites as grain-eating insects and rats. Human superorganisms prolifically bred unwanted weeds, vermin, worms, mosquitoes, fungi, bacteria, and viruses.

Hunter-gatherers—by staying dispersed and always moving on—avoided pileups of surpluses, garbage, and excrement, and thus did not attract and propagate these parasites. But even in the mild human concentrations of villages, tuberculosis, leprosy, and cholera soon appeared to darken our new existence. But it wasn't until we massed together in cities, however, that we provided the human concentrations that promoted continuous reinfections required by such vicious killers as smallpox and the bubonic plague. These parasites needed large, permanently emplaced concentrations of humans. Sumer contained the world's first large single-species stand of humans, as well as the first monocultures—solid stands of plants. It also boasted granaries chock full of food and the world's first riches of garbage. Rats, insects, and other pests had a field day on our dime.

The benefits of misery—the opportunists

Smallpox and measles infected essentially all citizens of Sumer when they were young; those lucky individuals who survived infancy were immune for life. Although many died young, they didn't carry a significant societal investment to their graves. Sumerians simply made up for their children's deaths by having more children. As these deaths were spread out over time, they had little effect other than immense human misery.

When Sumerian civilization came in contact with populations insufficiently large and dense to continually reinfect themselves, civilized diseases spread like wildfire through these non-immune populations, suddenly killing off young and old alike. The impact was devastating. Those left alive fell easy prey to the Sumerian armies, the very armies that had usually started the infections in the first place. Sumerians, with their nasty diseases, had a distinct survival advantage over their less civilized, disease-free neighbors.

This was Sumer's (temporarily) winning strategy: domesticate other species, exploit the land, breed like crazy, tax workers to bare subsistence, support as large an army as possible, and cultivate the worst possible diseases. This combination achieved growth ever outward from Sumer and other early centers of civilization, as humanity began its second great expansion around the globe. This time, instead of just large mammals and birds biting the dust, entire ecosystems crumbled. In our first expansion as top predator, the naïveté of large animals unaccustomed to spears led to their extinction. In our second expansion as superorganisms, the naïveté of entire ecosystems caused their own downfall. But how can entire ecosystems be naïve?

In forests, a tree occasionally falls, leaving a temporary opening to the sun, or a river cuts a new course, leaving the old river bed exposed. A special group of plants and animals, the opportunists, quickly move in and, as the trees eventually reclaim the land, then move on to new disruptions elsewhere in the normally serene forest. Ecologically, civilization is like a falling tree, a wayward river. It tears rents in the normal state of nature. But, rather than causing small, temporary, easily-healed disruptions scattered here and there, the onslaught of civilization is a continual, widespread disruption of natural systems via plowed fields, razed forests, overgrazed pastures, expanding cities, and monumental garbage heaps.

Now for the clever part: civilized humans, their domesticated animal partners, weeds, pests, and diseases—the whole lot—co-evolved in these continually disturbed environments. Disruption was like candy to them! The wholesale conversion of natural to human ecosystems had begun. Just as ant superorganisms out-competed solitary wasps, so too human civilizations pushed hunter-gatherers to the periphery.

This civilized combination, built on ecosystems in despair, first came to full flower in Mesopotamia about 3500 BC. Other civilizations began, for the most part independently, in Egypt (3100 BC), India (2000 BC), and China (2000 BC). Somewhat later on in the New World, civilizations which were completely independent from those in the Old World, emerged in both Mesoamerica and Peru.

Hydraulic civilizations

When humans took up sedentary agriculture, their available surpluses opened the door to civilization. These surpluses tended to be largest where soils were well suited to long periods of intensive agriculture. It's no coincidence that most civilizations began in river valleys where the rivers themselves periodically replenished the land with fresh nutrients. Most early civilizations were "hydraulic," based on the construction and maintenance of large-scale irrigation systems requiring central control and planning. The control of vital water supplies gave the authorities vast power. They maintained extensive lines of transportation and communication from governmental centers to the cities and, in turn, to the smallest villages. Political power ran in one direction, from top to bottom. Taxes and tributes flowed the opposite way. These hydraulic societies, in an age before powerful machines, depended on massed human labor to build and maintain their irrigation canals, roads, and other mammoth construction projects, such as the pyramids. With such ant-like armies of workers, it's little wonder that historians generally view these societies as despotic.

In hydraulic societies, the lives of farmers and construction laborers always hung just a notch above bare subsistence. Malnutrition and disease were rampant. The masses shared the same boat as their oxen, both subject to the commands of the small corps of elite who kept the records and managed society. Over time, corruption among the ruling class grew, public projects sat neglected, and canals filled with silt. Agricultural output eventually declined to the extent that it was no longer sufficient for the peasant masses. Starvation, internal revolt, or external conquerors would eventually bring a dynasty to its end. When new management restored canals and reduced corruption, hydraulic societies would struggle on again. In spite of the terrible human misery they caused, these hydraulic civilizations were stable, lasting for thousands of years, much longer than any others. This should give us pause. Ant-like forces within our own superorganisms may, unless we take great care, always have the upper hand over our chimpanzee individualistic values.

Sumer's fate

Although long lasting, a series of hydraulic societies—unless well situated indeed—couldn't last forever, as irreversible ecological damage eventually took its toll. The first signs of widespread ecological damage emerged in Mesopotamia—an area where extensive modifications to the natural environment had first been made. The intense irrigation agriculture of the Sumerians salted the Mesopotamian soil, and agricultural output eventually fell to a third of its record high. Since the Sumerians couldn't support vast armies anymore, they lost their empire. Sumer faded from memory as the encroaching sands covered the remains of humanity's first superorganisms. The city-states of Sumer had, in fact, been entirely forgotten until a couple of centuries ago when archaeologists began excavating some unusual mounds in the desert. They found thousands of clay tablets inscribed with a strange, archaic cuneiform script that they eventually decoded to reveal the earliest human civilization.

Sumer's sad end was hardly atypical; the archaeological record is a chronology of grand failures. Given the self-destructive process of deforestation, salination, and desertification, one cannot help but wonder why all complex civilizations haven't long since collapsed. Though civilizations have permanently ruined many environments, three temporary respites allowed them, at least up to our own age, to prosper nonetheless. These respites were technical developments that fostered: (1) expansion into fresh, undamaged territories; (2) the development of new energy sources that allowed us to profitably bring previously marginal land into production; and (3) transportation of food from areas of surplus to areas of scarcity. Although Sumer itself was doomed, its superorganism offspring and other independently-initiated civilizations haven't just stubbornly persisted for five thousand years, they've positively prospered.

The New World

The New World civilizations emerged late, even though, as in the Middle East, people lived and roamed the lands there some eleven thousand years ago, well before civilizations took off anywhere else on the globe. Anthropologists now believe that the main delay in the rise of New World civilizations stemmed from vital differences in the fauna and flora available for domestication.

In the New World, domesticatable herd animals had become extinct, either because of climatic change at the end of the last Ice Age or, more likely, through hunting. Similar animals weren't killed off in the Old World since, as mentioned earlier, they had millions of years to become wary of humans as we slowly improved our hunting capabilities. By contrast, animals in the New World simply had no time for such habituation. It took a mere thousand years from the time humans penetrated the continental ice-cap below Alaska for them to migrate, as the cap melted, all the way to the tip of South America, hunting the native fauna to extinction as they went. The only remaining large animals—the undomesticatable bison in North America—survived primarily because they weren't native. They were, in fact, savvy Old World animals that had arrived recently in the New World along with humanity.

The upshot of this situation was that no draft animals existed in the New World. New World humans also faced a meat shortage. Although they raised dogs and turkeys for meat (and guinea pigs in South America), all of these animals ate the same foods as humans. In the Old World, on the other hand, ruminants, which supplied most of the meat, ate grass and other food indigestible to humans—a significant advantage.

Another factor in the late start of New World civilizations was grains. American Indians had to domesticate maize instead of wheat. Although an excellent grain after many centuries of refinement (and now used by much of the Old World), maize (i.e., corn) was initially much more difficult and time consuming to domesticate than wheat.

So, in general, there was a dearth of easily domesticated plants and animals in the New World. Furthermore, the Americas lie in a north-south span, crossing many different climatic zones. This made it difficult for a species domesticated in one place to be useful in others. The Old World, where the first civilizations began, lies mainly in an east-west direction across somewhat similar climatic zones. Thus, migration, borrowing, and diffusion of domesticates may have been easier in the Old World. In spite of their late start, however, New World civilizations quickly flourished. The Maya erected large temple centers between 800 and 400 BC, and soon the New World boasted the largest cities on the planet.

Old meets new

While the outcome of the contest between civilizations and hunter-gatherers was never in doubt, the result of Old World civilizations meeting those in the New World is a more interesting story. Shortly after human hunter-gatherers arrived in the New World, rising oceans cut them off from their Asian homelands, as the dwindling Ice Age glaciers melted. This continental cutoff occurred after humans arrived, but before civilizations—Old World or New—began. Thus, Old and New World civilized ecosystems evolved separately for almost ten thousand years. They came into sudden and intimate contact five hundred years ago in a colossal ecological experiment.

Old World civilizations had a couple of thousand years' head start on the New World, so it's not surprising that they were the ones with ships and guns. Also, the Old World had large domesticated animals—Cortez arrived on horseback. The New World had no such advantages. Most importantly, the Old World had the nastiest civilized diseases, many of them developed from cohabitation with their large domesticated animals. Native Americans came to the New World before such Old World diseases had developed and remained, before Columbus, remarkably disease free (although the New World did donate syphilis to their Old World conquerors).

Old World civilizations—the successful teams of humans and their domesticated plants and animals—completed their planet-wide triumph on August 3, 1938, thus bringing to a close over one hundred thousand years of *Homo sapiens'* existence as an independent top predator. On this date, the advanced tentacles of the superorganisms that began in Sumer five thousand years earlier contacted the last remaining sizable group of hunter-gatherers. The Grand Central Valley of Papua New Guinea lay hidden by high mountains, surrounded by thick jungles, and undetected by the colonial settlements that had ringed the island's coastal areas for a century. The first pilot to fly over the central portion of the island was amazed to see over ten thousand campfires. Europeans, quickly hacking their way through the jungle, made the last first contact.

Chapter 7

MACHINES

The geese who laid the golden eggs

The tractor, unlike the horse, does not eat when not in use.
A machine can work tirelessly and uncomplainingly,
and can be scrapped rather than put on a pension.
Bruce Mazlish

For a list of all the ways technology has failed
to improve the quality of life, please press three.
Alice Khan

Machine evolution

Darwin's *Origin of Species* was published in 1859. He proposed that biological organisms evolved by processes of random mutation and natural selection. Just four years later, Samuel Butler asserted that machines had also developed in an evolutionary manner, one somewhat analogous to that of biological organisms. Both animals and machines convert energy into action. And, in both, we can discern long-term evolutionary trends towards ever more efficient use of energy and complexities of action. Butler, contrasting the speed at which machine evolution was progressing with the rate of biological evolution, boldly predicted that machines would, in due course, constitute a new class of life. He warned that machines would soon surpass us, relegating us—their human creators—to second-class status.

Historians of technology, such as George Basalla, emphasize the rarity of truly novel artifacts; each artifact by and large draws heavily on its predecessors. As with biological life, technological refinements accumulate evolutionarily; small improvements stacked on top of each other over time. As a result, we can trace an evolutionary tree—lines of descent—from the simplest tools to the most complex machines. This tree extends back only a couple of million years, however, instead of life's billions of years. Since *Homo sapiens* appeared on the scene, artifact diversity has grown so rapidly that it now rivals the diversity of life itself. There are, for instance, several million U.S. patents, just as there are several million animal species. And at least one major class of artifacts, the machines, consumes energy just as animals do. Machines, like life, have metabolisms. As Butler suggested, we ought to consider mechanical creations—especially machines—as another kingdom of life.

Life evolves, one generation to the next, by way of offspring variation and natural selection. Only the fittest survive and reproduce. Machines evolve, one generation to the next, because human designers produce a plethora of variations from which human users select the variants they find to be most capable, productive, and efficient. Only the most useful machines survive and multiply, forming the basis for a new round of variation, selection, and reproduction. Biological life adapts to its environment. Machines, on the other hand, remake their environments; felling forests, plowing fields, and damming rivers.

The pace of machine evolution is orders of magnitude faster than human genetic evolution, due both to human-introduced intentionality and the increasing widespread and rapid dissemination of extra-genetic information by way of spoken language, writing and, most recently, computers and the Internet. Human genes, by contrast, are selected without intentionality. They inevitably evolve slowly because genetic information can be disseminated only to one's own offspring and, at that, only one human generation at a time.

Westside story

Until recently, civilizations were supported by the hard labor of peasants or slaves. Humans, for the most part, provided the brute force it took to grind grain, cut wood, and raise water to irrigate fields. Then, starting almost a thousand years ago, civilization based on non-human power arose in Western Europe. It relied primarily on water power—supplemented by wind and animal power—to accomplish tasks formerly performed by human serfs or slaves. Sophisticated waterwheels captured the motive power of running water, enabling an increasing number of cleverly designed machines to grind grain, saw boards, and irrigate crops, as well as accomplish numerous other labor-intensive tasks. The *Domesday Book* (1086), compiled by the Norman conquerors of England, lists more than five thousand water mills in southern England alone, almost one for every fifty households. Windmills, from the twelfth century on, sprouted up like spring flowers throughout all of Western Europe.

Why was the West a particularly fertile ground for proliferation of these water- and wind-driven machines? Why did the West encourage the evolution of machine life? Why were the often illiterate peasants of Northern Europe more favorably inclined towards facilitating the evolution of machines as compared to their predecessors, the well-educated and highly refined intellectuals of classic Greece and Rome? Three causes have been suggested: (1) a pragmatic down-to-earth attitude, (2) decentralized governments, and (3) stiff economic and military competition between the countries of Western Europe.

The first of these three is the suggestion that the pragmatic attitude of the West was a cause of Northern Europe's favorable inclination towards the evolution of machines. In classic civilizations, the educated elite rarely lowered themselves to do the physical work involved in day-to-day living, relegating such mere practicalities to their slaves. In early medieval Europe, after the demise of the Roman Empire, the only intellectuals left were the monks. Given the origins of Roman Christianity in the lower classes of society, it's not surprising that monks believed that physical labor directed towards practical ends, far from being degrading, was actually virtuous. As St. Benedict might have suggested, weeding the garden also frees the soul of weeds. Nor were the Western Christians reticent about reaping the rewards from nature that practical work could yield; Thomas Aquinas voiced the widespread Christian belief that nature's very purpose was to serve humanity. Thus, manipulating nature for economic gain was virtuous—by doing so we helped God implement His plan. The practical West assertively pursued material progress with a religious, missionary zeal.

The pragmatism of the West also had no sense of shame when it came to adopting foreign ideas—whatever worked. Medieval technology was carried forward by practical peasants, stonemasons, lumberjacks, and miners with the modest intent of bettering their humble existence. Unlike other civilized traditions, which discouraged novelty, thinking it evil, the West, particularly during and after the Renaissance, actively sought out fresh ideas. Designing fanciful variations on existing machines became a respectable intellectual occupation pursued by dreamers who thought up novel, often physically unrealizable machines. Leonardo da Vinci (1452-1519) was the epitome of the playful, intellectual creator of such "paper machines," most of which could not be realized—at least in his day.

The second factor contributing to the West's fertile environment for the evolution of machines was its decentralized governments. Innovators are, almost by definition, eccentric people. Innovation is more likely to flourish in those societies which tolerate nonconformity. Strong, centralized governments devote themselves to the status quo, to a conservative conformity that stifles creativity. Looser, decentralized governments—while not necessarily encouraging novelty—are at least less hostile towards the eccentric. Unlike the hydraulic societies of the Near East and Asia, Europeans—who depended on rain, not irrigation, for water—had less need to centralize. After the demise of the highly centralized and autocratic Roman Empire, landed nobles and cities successfully resisted large-scale recentralization. Pluralistic societies emerged, composed of relatively autonomous spheres of politics, religion, education, arts, and commerce. Soon these pluralistic societies curtailed the rights of kings and centralized governments; witness, for example, the signing of the Magna Carta.

Finally, and of utmost significance for the swift evolution of machines, Europe remained divided into a number of decidedly competitive states. Competition was not only military, but economic. National leaders understood that hostility towards innovation eventually translated into economic and, in due course, military loss. Thus, the more astute European countries directly encouraged innovation by way of patents, grants, prizes, and medals. Although irate Luddite mobs occasionally burned books and smashed machines, as long as a few European countries remained creative, the others, in order to survive, were forced to follow.

Capitalism and creativity

What emerged in Western Europe was the free enterprise system—capitalism. Governments no longer set prices or controlled production and distribution; individuals and firms were given the freedom to make these decisions. Prior to capitalism, the elite gained prominence through governmental, military, or ecclesiastical careers. The brightest, most capable, and well-educated elite shunned low-class economic activities. Increasingly, however, merchants—who produced and distributed the goods of daily life—gained prominence based on their considerable accumulations of wealth. Merchants in Holland and England soon dominated their parliaments. These two countries, Holland and England, were early leaders in the accumulation of mercantile wealth.

The capitalists who received the most generous financial rewards were those, in the best of Western traditions, who improved the lifestyles of the numerous poor as opposed to the wealthy few. Economic power resides with the masses. Not only did technical advances benefit the masses, they simultaneously penalized the rich company owners whose outmoded production techniques were being displaced, their investments and livelihoods ruined. Most traditional societies protected such vested interests, suppressing innovations to maintain the status quo. In the highly competitive West, on the other hand, governments were anxious to spur economic progress, so they protected creative minds from the retaliation of their rich and powerful victims whose businesses often failed in the face of new technologies. The upshot: firms that successfully brought their inventions or services to market often achieved astounding overnight success. Those who failed to innovate, who rested on their laurels, faced severe penalties. It's hard to imagine a more fertile ground for rapidly expanding trade and for the swift evolution of machines.

Eastside story (Far East that is)

Western civilization was now poised to make its planetary bid. But why hadn't China, which was for centuries the most technically advanced civilization on Earth, already taken this path? China was, after all, the first civilization to develop the essential components of modern technology. China's sophisticated utilization of iron, clever machines (such as clocks driven by water power), and books printed from skillfully carved wooden blocks—not to mention its invention of rockets and other marvels—speak to its ample creativity.

The Chinese, unlike the environmentally exploitative and aggressive Westerners, stressed harmony between humanity and nature, as well as harmony within their unified kingdom. Evolution thrives on competition, not harmony. The Chinese weren't goaded by constant competition from other countries and had no need to wring every last possible economic advantage from their unquestioned inventiveness. The story of Admiral Chen Ho is illustrative.

A hundred years before Columbus, the Chinese constructed a fleet of seagoing junks that dwarfed any vessels Europeans had ever built. With an army of thousands aboard, Admiral Ho's fleet voyaged as far as Africa. But rather than establishing trade, the Chinese turned inwards again when the Emperor issued a decree that seagoing junks with more than two masts were forbidden. Soon, the shipyards were closed.

The West's response to the voyages of Columbus and other early explorers could not have been more different. In the competitive West, the scramble was on to build ships, claim new territories for the mother countries (while completely ignoring the rights of the indigenous populations), and extract as much wealth from the new lands as possible. The Spanish went directly for the gold, while the ever-practical English planted cotton in Virginia and the other colonies of the American South.

King Cotton

Although the use of water-powered machines to refine linen and wool had increased in England in the early eighteenth century, it was the processing of cotton into finished fabrics that shifted the evolution of machines into high gear. Cotton, compared to linen or wool, provides better ventilation, washes easily, and absorbs dyes and printed patterns well. Cotton is also relatively undemanding to grow. All these qualities gear cotton toward mass, low-class consumption. The difficulty with cotton, however, was that it took an exorbitant fifty thousand hours of human work to spin one hundred pounds of cotton by hand, and even then, the result was of low strength and poor quality.

In 1764, James Hargreaves invented the spinning jenny, a machine that could spin low-grade cotton. Samuel Crompton came out with the "mule" in 1779, and it spun cotton thread that was finer, stronger, and more uniform than the best linen or wool. It took the mule just three hundred hours to spin one hundred pounds of cotton. Finally, in 1785, Edmund Cartwright's power loom transformed cotton thread into fabric, completing the mechanization of cotton textile production.

Cotton exploded. The forested lands of America's southern colonies were transformed overnight into immense plantations that raised cotton, a plant originally native to Egypt, Asia, and Mexico. The United States imported millions of slaves from Africa to tend these plantations. A constant stream of ships moved countless bales of cotton across the Atlantic to the factories that sprang up along the fast-running streams and rivers of northern England. As the sole supplier of low cost but high quality cotton textiles to the world, England became increasingly wealthy.

The cheapest labor on Earth couldn't compete with the English cotton machines. The English found it was more economical to grow Indian cotton in the southern American colonies (Virginia, the Carolinas, and Georgia), transport it all the way across the Atlantic to mills on England's west coast, and then ship the resultant finished cloth to India for sale than it was to raise Indian cotton in India and use the planet's cheapest manual labor to spin it into thread and weave it into fabric. Machines are powerful. Machines are fast. Machines never rest. And the transportation cost—at least of high value goods—is not all that high. It was a simple matter of machine efficiency and economics. Of course, for this to continue to work for them, the English could not allow their precious cotton-producing machines to operate in America, let alone in India.

Besides the West's innovative spirit and capitalistic zeal, there were two additional keys to the industrial revolution: (1) machines that made machines, and (2) a ready supply of low cost, compliant labor. The industrial revolution simply wouldn't have been possible without machines that built machines. Lathes, milling machines, and screw-cutting machines transformed designs into a precise, replicable, metallic reality; machine life had inspired its own peculiar means of reproduction. The essence of the industrial revolution was, after all, the widespread substitution of high-productivity machines for low-productivity humans.

But humans could not be dispensed with entirely. Not yet automatic, machines required human tenders. Machines churned out textiles and other goods at a prodigious rate. It took a virtual army of hard working, on-the-spot people to tend the machines and keep them fully supplied. Unlike the leisurely, humane pace of cottage industry production prior to mechanization, tending machines was a frenzied, inhumane activity. The age of factories had commenced.

Noisy and dirty, factories demanded long hours of mind-numbing, repetitive labor by workers who soon numbered in the millions. Although the factories' owners offered incredibly low wages, they always had ample recruits because fewer workers were needed in the increasingly efficient English agricultural system. Their eagerness to work in the dismal city factories speaks volumes for the lot of those who were still unemployed in the countryside. Similar to the farmers at the dawn of agriculture, their choice was between hard work and starvation. The new elite—this time the rich capitalists—drove humanity towards maximal work. It would be a hundred years before the rapidly growing factories brought full employment and hence sufficient worker scarcity to boost wages to a level that provided factory hands with a decent living.

Steam power

For all the successes of water power, it had significant limitations; water power was, after all, at the mercy of droughts, floods, and ice. In any event, water power could be tapped only alongside the sizable and fast-moving streams, and the banks of these streams were rapidly filled up with factories. A new motive power for the machines was clearly required.

It was England's good fortune to sit atop a virtual mountain of coal. Coal had occasionally been used in England for heat, light, and even cooking, but folks considered it inferior to wood, owing to its noxious fumes and grimy soot. England used little coal until the forests were virtually gone; then coal use soared, especially for heating. The English rapidly exhausted the supply of easily accessed surface coal and began to extract it from ever-deepening mines. A serious problem with such mines, however, was the considerable effort required to pump out the water that incessantly seeped into their deep shafts.

This brings us to Thomas Newcomen and the first useful machines that produced motive power by burning fossil fuel. In 1712, Newcomen's coal-fed "atmospheric" engines began pumping water from the coal mines. That date marks the beginning of the fossil-fuel machine age. Large, cumbersome, and inefficient, Newcomen's engines quickly gave way to more compact, versatile steam engines, devised by that quintessential mechanical genius, James Watt. In next to no time, steam engines replaced water power as the prime motive force for England's rapidly growing manufacturing industry.

Early in the nineteenth century, when steam engines were just beginning to see widespread use, coal consumption still hovered at a tiny fraction of what it was to become. Then Richard Trevithick took a major step forward with his refinement of the steam engine. Trevithick operated his engines at a pressure of ten atmospheres, which Watt—who used less than two atmospheres—considered dangerously high. Trevithick's compact, high-pressure steam engines proved to be safe, however, and more energy efficient than Watt's machines, extracting more work from a ton of coal. In 1804, a Trevithick steam engine powered a locomotive that hauled itself, ten tons of iron bar, and seventy cheering passengers along a nine-mile tramway, winning a 500-guinea wager. From this modest beginning, steam-powered railroads—over the course of the nineteenth century—opened up the interiors of vast continents to the English, other European, and American locomotives, the most dearly beloved of all fossil fuel machines.

Soon European and American steamships plied the planet's oceans, while their expanding factories produced material goods in great abundance. Lighted by low-cost coal gas, factories kept a rapidly expanding industrial workforce busy in dingy, machine-filled rooms long after natural darkness. By the end of the nineteenth century, steam power reigned supreme. Coal use had soared to a record 95% of the now greatly expanded human energy consumption, completely dwarfing all other sources of power including wind, human, and animal. The age of fossil-fuel machines had arrived full force.

It is instructive to consider the similarities between the coming of the age of fossil-fuel machines and the onset of the earliest photosynthetic life. By tapping coal, steam engines initiated a novel metabolic process, pioneering the use of a previously unexploited source of energy—in this case coal rather than sunlight. Over a billion years earlier, photosynthetic life had a field day when it tapped the limitless energy of the sun, generating an explosion of activity and new forms, polluting the planet with waste oxygen, and generally running out of control. Nor were the photosynthetic upstarts ever brought to heel; other life had to adjust to the new photosynthetic world order. Now, coal-eating steam machines followed suit, running rampant, massively polluting, and changing the planet, perhaps forever (or at least having a decent go at it). Steam machines, however, were but a precursor of things to come.

The usefulness of steam-powered machines was limited by the difficulty of transporting their bulky fuel—coal—long distances from mines, as well as by the large size and slow startup of these coal-fired machines. The value of coal as a source of energy soared yet again, however, with the dawn of the electrical age in the late nineteenth century. Electricity was responsible for a substantial increase in the power consumed by humans or, more accurately, by their machines. Electricity emerged as a convenient source of power for both large and small applications, though its use was constrained to fixed locations where power lines could connect to distant massive electric generators turned by coal-fired steam turbines.

Those infernal combustion machines

Coal-eating steam machines were just the first wave of fossil-fuel-powered machines to sweep the planet. Although coal-fired steam engines rightly claimed responsibility for the phenomenal success of the railroads, such engines weren't as practical for drawing plows through fields or for hauling people or light loads short distances. Thus, somewhat paradoxically, as steam railroad transport increased in the late nineteenth century, so did the use of horse-drawn plows, combines, carriages, and wagons. Horse ownership peaked in both England and in United States early in the twentieth century. In 1900, an amazing one-third of the farmland in the United States was devoted to growing food for horses. Removing their waste from the streets of cities and towns became a major occupation, and people complained incessantly about the offensive pollution. The stage was set for the replacement of both horse-powered agricultural machines and horse-drawn, short-haul transport. In their stead, machines powered with petroleum burning internal combustion engines came to the fore. Unlike coal, the residue of ancient forests, oil was the gift of ancient unicellular sea life. Solid coal had to be laboriously mined. Liquid oil could be conveniently pumped. Now and then it even squirted out of the ground of its own accord.

While urbanites understand, first hand, the revolutionary impact of internal combustion engines on short-distance human travel, from a broader perspective, the impact of these engines on agriculture was even more profound. Chain saws and bulldozers cleared and leveled vast areas of land for agricultural use. Gasoline and diesel powered engines pumped water to irrigate formerly non-arable land. Farmers used petroleum powered machines in all phases of the agricultural cycle: tractors pulled the plows that prepared fields, specialized machines planted seeds, and other machines tended growing plants and harvested mature crops. Oil burning machines transported the harvest to railheads or to distant final markets. In 1812, machines began placing food into the sealed, tin-plated cans invented by Peter Druand. Internal combustion vehicles carried fertilizers and other raw materials back to the farm, including refined fossil petroleum products for the rapidly proliferating farm machines. As petroleum-fired equipment took over the main work of agriculture, it freed millions of humans from agricultural labor, enabling them to tend the ever-growing number of machines in the factories.

Machine virtues

Human hunter-gatherers were clever enough to stop working once they'd gathered enough to eat. Collecting enough food to sustain themselves in just a few hours, they had generous time for social activities or just relaxing in the cool shade. With the advent of agriculture, however, the majority of humans spent their waking hours—shoulder to the plow—slaving away in the hot sun.

The real problem with farmers, though, was that even when they worked hard all day long, they produced a disappointingly small surplus. Traditional agriculture—in terms of food produced per working hour—was much less labor efficient than hunting and gathering because farmers had to do so many additional things besides gathering the end results. They had to clear the land, plant the seeds, keep the weeds down ... the list goes on and on. Only by working all day long could farmers produce more food than hunter-gatherers could kill or glean in a few hours.

Owing to the relative inefficiency of agriculture, pre-mechanized civilizations found it necessary, on average, for some 90% of their people to work full time at farming in order to support themselves and the non-farming 10%. And even then, only a small portion of the non-farmers were the real elites who truly benefited from this small surplus. The elite couldn't be numerous, because agriculture based on human work just wasn't very efficient. Let's face it: humans, even when you work them to the bone, still eat a lot and keep getting out of line. They are a weak and unruly lot if there ever was one!

Machines are refreshingly different. A hundred, or even a thousand times stronger than a human, the more recent and powerful machines eat readily available fossil fuels, delight in working twenty-four hours a day, and don't require a police force to keep them in line. One could extol the civilized virtues of machines at length, but the most revealing contrast between humans and machines is simply this: machines, unlike humans, naturally generate very large surpluses. Machines opened the door of hope for the huddled masses yearning for the good life.

The golden age of plenty

Over the past hundred years, industrial production has increased by an astounding factor of fifty, most of it since 1950. We owe this primarily to the hard work of our machine partners. The increase is also due, in part, to our adaptation of industrial mass production techniques. The industrial mass production revolution began with interchangeable rifle parts in the American Civil War, and came to full fruition with the manufacture of that black, mobile, petroleum-eating machine known simply as the Model T.

Henry Ford used powerful machines not only to overcome human frailties, but to simplify the human jobs that remained, creating the industrial assembly line. Humans, in a sense, became machines themselves. With mass-production industry, as with mass-production agriculture, output soared as the number of workers declined, replaced in both cases by a growing number of ever-more-efficient machines. The vast ranks of people released from agriculture and then from industry, were employed in the "third sector," providing human services to the increasingly affluent industrial societies.

Once machines took over the main work of agriculture, the acreage the average farmer could manage increased dramatically as the number of farms plummeted. Agricultural output skyrocketed, even as fewer and fewer people worked on farms. The original dream of agriculture, of civilization itself, had finally been realized after a mere five thousand years. Agricultural civilizations had finally emerged that could produce more food per hour of human work than could the hunter-gatherers who'd preceded them. Civilized humans could now, at long last, be better off than their hunter-gatherer ancestors. The masses could, at least in theory, become as wealthy and well fed as the elite of yore, all because fossil-fuel burning machines had taken over the hard work, the real labor.

Formerly, some 90% of the humans in civilizations had farmed to support the other 10%. Today, in most industrialized countries, fewer than 10% are farmers; they feed the more than 90% who aren't. In Australia, as an extreme example, one farmer (and his extensive collection of machine partners) supports, on average, 125 people—83 of them overseas. Such farming effectiveness became possible only because we tapped into a new source of energy—oil. We are, to an incredible extent, increasingly "eating" oil.

The fact that the majority of the people in today's industrial societies are well fed and healthy—with more than adequate housing, clothing, and other basic necessities—is a stunning achievement for humanity and our machine partners. Since civilization began, the bulk of humanity has, until recently, been consigned to lives of grinding poverty just this side of starvation. The sudden turn of good fortune in the industrialized civilizations, which began some two hundred years ago, was a fortuitous confluence of four factors: (1) we found large and highly productive areas of new land in the Americas, Australia, and New Zealand; (2) efficient machines burning fossil fuels took over most of the hard work; (3) we institutionalized and refined the mass production techniques that machines and fossil fuels made possible in both agriculture and industry; and (4) of greatest importance, all these things happened suddenly, boosting the supply of food and manufactured goods faster than the growth of the populations of industrialized nations.

Machine dominance

Humanity's shift from hunting and gathering to agriculture was virtually worldwide, as was the shift to civilization. Those who shifted first tended to dominate the others. The manufacture and use of coal-fired machines during the nineteenth century was, at first, restricted to England and a few other western European countries. Although the United States and Japan soon joined in, most of the world remained pre-industrial, which was advantageous to the industrial countries. By controlling the manufacture of the surplus producing, fossil-fuel-burning machines, the West and Japan could effectively control the planet and keep colonies in a pre-industrial, agricultural state—often with the able help of natives trained at the universities of the colonial powers. Colonies could be obliged to supply food and raw materials, transported by machine-powered trains and ships to the industrial countries that consumed the food and processed the raw materials in factories powered by fossil-fuel machines. The colonial powers then shipped back a small portion of the finished products to their colonies to "pay" for the food and raw materials. What a deal!

Civilizations have always had their ruling elite; now the planet had its ruling civilizations. A few countries controlled the others, working them hard, extracting their surpluses and, as is the way of all biologically efficient parasites, giving little in return. In some cases, these "elite" countries gained control through settlement, out reproducing the sparsely populated natives whose numbers were reduced by both guns and civilized diseases. At other times, they seized control by military force or the raw economic power born of machine-produced surpluses.

At the height of the Victorian Age, nineteenth-century England epitomized industrialized civilization. She extracted resources from her widespread colonies and dependencies. She supported her merchants and industrial barons in their commercial endeavors with a naval steamship force and coaling stations throughout the world. She even shipped herself food from Australia and New Zealand. To pay her providers, England sent back a few manufactured goods, not to mention surplus, unwanted people. With the invention of refrigerated ships in 1876, England and other European nations could enjoy year-round fresh meat, butter, and even tropical fruit from abroad. The population of Europeans grew rapidly, both at home and in their colonies. Their mastery of machinery multiplied the impact of their rapidly growing numbers.

Machines reign supreme

As we enter the new millennium, machines and their capitalist masters reign supreme. Communism, which was the only real challenge to capitalism, has fallen on self-induced hard times. Real communism works well for the altruistic ants, but not so well for somewhat selfish chimpanzees. A growing number of capitalistic emulators have joined the West, and several are beating it at its own game—the mechanized production of vast quantities of goods. The latest wave of self-controlled machines—robots—is concentrated in a single country, Japan. And China has become the planet's factory.

As global transportation and communication have improved, as capitalistic Western ways have permeated the entire planet, the economic competition that began between European states has become increasingly global. The power of governments to control the economy, never very strong in the West, is now totally overshadowed by both the size and the logic of production efficiency inherent in the mechanized global economy.

Thanks to our machine partners, we in the West now accomplish our chores at the touch of a button. We have, at last, entered the Golden Age only dreamed of heretofore. We luxuriate in a sea of machine-produced goods. But, our rapidly proliferating chainsaws and bulldozers are consuming the planet's last forests. A vast army of machines are filling the air, water, and land with their effluents. It is gradually dawning on a few of us, the chimpanzees who would be ants, that perhaps we might have been had. Machines, initially few, gained our confidence as our faithful servants. We gladly helped them evolve and proliferate. We even promoted them to nearly full partnership. But now the tables may be turning. Are machines enslaving us, and consuming the planet to boot? Ralph Waldo Emerson summed up this worry in 1847 (*The Channing Ode*).

> Things are in the saddle,
> And ride mankind.
> There are two laws discrete,
> Not reconciled,—

Law for man, and law for thing;
The last builds town and fleet,
But it runs wild,
And doth the man unking.

Ironically, although these lines are often quoted by those decrying the evils of industrialization, few quotes also include the lines that immediately follow:

'Tis fit the forest fall,
The steep be graded,
The mountain tunneled,
The sand shaded,
The orchard planted,
The glebe tilled,
The prairie granted,
The steamer built.
Let man serve law for man.

Although we love our machines, every silver lining has its cloud.

Chapter 8

SCIENTISTS
The curious cats who pried open Pandora's Box

I would contend that if something
fits in with common sense
it almost certainly isn't science.
If scientific ideas were natural,
they would not have required the difficult and
protracted techniques of science for their discovery.
Lewis Wolpert

When dealing with nature,
one cannot easily or long evade reality.
Henry Bauer

The social roots of science

Who are we? How did we come to be? These are the persistent questions of young children, inebriated college students philosophizing late on Friday night, and those academics we call scientists. As a stellar astronomer, I number myself among the impractical scientists, pleased with the total lack of any earthly utility in the observations I record and analyze of a few eclipsing binaries. Thankfully, I belong to a tiny minority. If we were all scientists, the crops would rot, our machines would fall into disrepair, and civilization itself would grind to a halt for lack of practical attention.

For the last four hundred years, scientists have been on an unbroken, collective quest to understand who we are and how we came to be. Although humans have always been curious, only recently has our curiosity led to the cooperative, wholesale prying into nature that is the hallmark of modern science. What changed? Why did modern science arise in the crude West instead of in the more intellectually sophisticated civilizations of China or the Islamic world? And for that matter, why should any animal, including us, ask about its nature or origins, let alone struggle so long to find answers?

The chimpanzees, our sister species, are keenly aware of the personalities, current emotions, and motives of others in their group. They keep a careful, day-to-day account of the complex and ever-shifting interrelationships among their comrades. Experts at social chess, they have a highly evolved Machiavellian intelligence. They're equipped with mental models of themselves in relation to the other chimpanzees around them and can, to a limited extent, project ahead.

We humans have taken this mental modeling further than our sister chimpanzees, although scientists who work with chimps admit to being frequently suckered by their tricks. Humans not only have the advantage of a larger brain with a more extensive memory, we have also developed a much more complex and expressive language that, besides improving communication, also assists us in our mental modeling of complex social realities.

It is normal during human development to infuse non-living things with human purposefulness. The famous French developmental psychologist, Jean Piaget, called this animism, and it is particularly evident in children between the ages of two and four. Animism is an over-generalization of a child's early realization that some objects (such as other humans) have mental states. Hunter-gatherers also believed that many inanimate objects, such as trees and rocks, possessed human-like spirits. To make sense of physical forces such as weather, hunter-gatherers logically gave these forces human or animal-like attributes—endowing most of nature with emotions, motives, and purposes. In this, and in our early animistic religions, we projected our social-chess mental model onto the physical and biological world around us. It was the natural, inevitable thing for us to do. Our mental models were developed for understanding and predicting human behavior, so they are not entirely applicable to the behavior of other animals, let alone physical processes. However, one does the best one can with what one has.

Ancient science

With early civilizations, religion became organized and central to human life. We had no idea of our lengthy, prehistoric, evolutionary past, so early priest-kings suggested, logically enough, that we were the remnants of a previous Golden Age, and that we (especially the priest-kings) were descended from the gods. Most myths looked back with nostalgia to a golden past, to a lost Garden of Eden. The universe is capricious, and only the constant intercession of priests asking special favors of the gods could forestall further degradation. Early written religions grew in eloquence and detail, linking nature and gods to increasingly sophisticated, comprehensive, human-centered explanations. Understandably, priests made no confessions of ignorance or lack of understanding. There was no critical tradition.

Some twenty-five centuries ago, a few elite Greeks received license to pursue, within tasteful bounds, lines of inquiry that departed from traditionally religious ones, and to openly critique each other's ideas. By substituting reason for traditional religious explanations, these skeptical Greek inquirers made significant contributions to explaining the natural world. The Greeks, for example, transformed a collection of various practical rules of calculation into orderly systems of thought. The most famous of these, Euclid's *Elements,* remains useful to this day. With geometric reasoning, the Greek scholars proposed that the Earth was round and, based on relatively simple measurements, estimated its diameter with considerable accuracy.

Mathematics and early science flowered with the Greeks, though they relied on logical deduction, having little use for practical, get-your-hands-dirty experimentation. The Greeks demonstrated that human brains, despite evolving as aids to survival and propagation in a social environment, could be successfully used to ferret out obscure cosmic realities in an appropriately open and critical setting.

The Christians who followed the Greeks in the West were not kindly disposed toward the non-human-centered viewpoints of the ancient Greek philosophers. The Christians destroyed (or carelessly lost) many of the Greek classics. Thanks to individual Islamic scholars, however, the unusual Greek insights into a non-human oriented but true-to-nature reality were preserved. Islamic religion required its scholars to treat the Greek views as foreign, thus defending their own religious beliefs against the invasion of an alien philosophy with incompatible views. Nevertheless, Islamic scholars were allowed to study the Greek classics of philosophy and science. Going well beyond studying, they made many brilliant contributions of their own, such as Arabic numerals and the systemization of algebra. The Islamic world, however, did not pursue the Greek line of thought in any vigorous manner, even banning its teaching from institutions of higher learning.

The Chinese, with the largest and most successful civilization in the world, had an extensive educational system for training their bureaucracy. China printed large quantities of books hundreds of years before printing began in the West. Their education emphasized literary classics that accentuated the worthy social ethic of living together in harmony. Entry to the higher levels of government required extensive knowledge of this literature—especially of the Confucian classics. The Chinese revered ancient wisdom.

Brimming with technological genius, China maintained a carefully balanced, albeit somewhat human-centered point of view. Humanity and nature, they reasoned, should peacefully coexist. Life is a never-ending cycle, and the key to life for them was maintaining harmony and balance at all times.

Western discourse

The Christian West's predominant view, St. Francis and other lovers of nature aside, was radically different. Humans were separate, above nature, for only we had souls. We had no obligation to the soulless lower animals; nature existed to serve us. Nature, far from being animated with independent spirits that were capricious and unpredictable, had an underlying,

Can Nancy's Story Connect w/ Gaia?

God-given order. These Christian-inspired beliefs led to a detached, objective, and rather mechanical view of nature. From the Christian, Western point of view, nature didn't have any mind or soul of its own, so tinkering with it was neither sacrilegious nor dangerous. Furthermore, Christianity saw the Earth as the stage for a divine play—a play that had a definite beginning, a one-way story line, and an eventual end—certainly not the cyclic, endless nature many other cultures had envisioned.

Having lost the Greek scientific classics, Christianized Western Europe had no need to erect barriers against these powerful alien thoughts. By the time they were translated from Arabic in the twelfth and thirteenth centuries, the West was ready for them. Roman law and Christian theology had laid a foundation for believing that humans were rational beings, that public discourse had considerable value. Such discourse had already led to the scholarly disciplines of jurisprudence and theology. In addition, the West had inherited a religion, Christianity, which was actively persecuted by the state, at least initially. As a result, the church fought for and eventually obtained its own rights, separate from those of the state. Merchants, following the church's lead, also secured many rights of their own.

Within this social and intellectual atmosphere, the universities of Europe arose—scholarly guilds that had the right (as did other guilds) to conduct their own affairs as they saw fit, without undue interference from either the state or established religion. By 1200, two of the earliest universities, Oxford and Paris, based much of their curricula on Greek science—preserved by the Islamic world and recently translated into Latin. A statute enacted in 1255 by the entire Faculty of Arts at Paris directed that all students read Aristotle's natural science books, even specifying the time to be spent reading them. Paris examined all students on their knowledge of Aristotelian logic and science. The view of the universe as an ordered system understandable by humans soon prevailed in the West.

Many scholars were convinced that continuing the rational discourse among competing ideas would eventually lead to ever greater understanding. This discourse, begun by the Greeks two thousand years earlier, was renewed in the West as a growing number of disputed questions in physics, astronomy, and other disciplines were earnestly and openly debated. The Masters prepared scholarly reviews of various questions and answers, which their students studied and debated. Does the Earth turn on its axis? Is there a vacuum? Can things happen by chance? These were the hot topics of the day.

The states not only allowed but even supported institutions that encouraged free inquiry, chartering scholars to develop the most consistent and theoretically powerful explanatory systems. Free inquiry was supported even though it was realized that the fruits of such quests would not always be to the liking of the state, let alone the church. Although individual European states would at times renege, squelching academic freedom and scientific inquiry, the West as a whole was committed to freedom of thought for the same reason it was committed to mercantile freedom: competition.

The origins of modern science

Modern science was the result, to a significant extent, of the efforts of two men near the beginning of the seventeenth century: the Italian mathematician Galileo and the English barrister Francis Bacon. Unlike Greek scientists, who two thousand years earlier had shunned hands-on experimentation, Galileo insisted on the empirical testing of theories. Aristotle had claimed, on logically deductive grounds, that heavy objects fall faster than lighter ones. Galileo subjected Aristotle's claim to empirical test. Tradition has Galileo simultaneously dropping two balls of different weight from the Leaning Tower of Pisa. They both hit the ground at the same time, thus overturning Aristotle's erroneous deduction. In so doing, Galileo brought into question all purely deductive, intuitively logical explanations not backed by actual experimental verification. A mathematician, Galileo looked for and found a mathematical order underlying his empirical observations.

After hearing rumors that newly developed lenses could make distant objects appear closer, Galileo built, in 1609, the first astronomical telescope. Using it to discover and study the moons of Jupiter and the phases of Venus, he provided convincing support for Copernicus's theory that the Earth orbited the Sun, not *vice versa*. Just months after turning his telescope to the heavens, Galileo, at his own expense, published his observational results in a book. Not wishing to be scooped, he had some five hundred copies of *The Sidereal Messenger* delivered to influential figures throughout Europe. Shutting the barn door after the horses had left, the Church put an aging Galileo on trial for heresy. Keeping in mind the recent fate of Giordano Bruno, who was burned at the stake in 1600, for similar heresies, Galileo recanted his assertion that the Earth moves around the Sun. Legend has it, however, that as they pronounced sentence on him, Galileo unrepentantly mumbled, "Yet it moves."

The primary effect of the Church's action against Galileo was to place a chill on Italian and Southern European science. Protestant Northern Europe might also have dealt modern science an early blow, had it not been for Francis Bacon. An experienced barrister in Queen Elizabeth's government and a vocal publicist, Bacon championed the idea that science glorified God by reading His book of nature. God intended, Bacon suggested, that we should have dominion over the planet, and science could provide us with the power we needed to take our rightful place in the scheme of things. Through knowledge built up via science's methodical investigations of nature, we could progress towards a new Golden Age.

Far from being sacrilegious or heretical, Bacon assured everyone, science served God, revealed His truth, and allowed us to help Him achieve His ends. Francis Bacon's championing of science led directly to the founding of England's Royal Society, the first organization totally dedicated to science. In competitive Northern Europe, science had found an appreciative home. The science genie was out of the bottle and neither the West nor the planet could ever put it back again.

The nature of modern science

The Greeks had attempted to obtain total certitude by way of reason and pure logic. This could be done without stooping to lower-class practicalities, thus neatly matching their elitist attitudes. But, as Galileo demonstrated with his free-falling weights, logic without empirical verification could easily lead one astray, producing unreliable, even false, information. Although modern science, like Greek science, still insists on logical, often mathematical consistency, its primary criterion for reliability was empirical verification, usually via clever demonstrations—experiments that showed the claimed results to be the actual case. Only after other scientists independently confirmed these demonstrations did the scientific community accept the results. Unlike the Greeks, modern science made no claims with respect to absolute certainty, simply adopting the most comprehensive and reliable explanation proffered, always open to reconsideration in light of new empirical evidence or a better theory.

The genius of the modern scientific process was that it allowed reliable information and understandings to accumulate without everyone having to prove everything for themselves. No re-invention of the wheel. Because one could generally count on the results of other scientists (once replicated) to be reliable, one could concentrate one's own efforts on one small piece of science's overall collective effort. There could be almost as many specialties as there were scientists.

For modern science to work its magic, however, all the participants had to adhere to a rather strict understanding as to what did and did not constitute reliable knowledge. Those who did not toe the line were quickly marginalized by peers, though not usually burned at the stake. Appeals to religious authority, spiritual revelation, widespread public belief, pure logic, human comfort, or economic advantage were all rejected out of hand as unreliable. Only empirically verifiable and logically consistent explanations were accepted, and then only provisionally. Explanations were always open to being discredited by new experiments or replaced by more comprehensive or cleverly-crafted explanations.

To protect themselves from unreliable information contaminating their primary vehicle of communications—their journals—scientists instituted a screening process based on peer review. Beginning with the *Proceedings of the Royal Society*, recognized experts in a given area reviewed proposed papers, rejecting them if they could not be brought up to prevailing scientific standards. Science isn't about freedom of the press, it's about a collective enterprise for the accumulation of reliable information. "The West alone," as Nathan Rosenberg and L. E. Birdzell noted, "succeeded in getting a large number of scientists, specialized by different disciplines, to cooperate in creating an immense body of tested and organized knowledge whose reliability could be accepted by all scientists."

But science isn't just an accumulation of verifiable "facts." It is also an accumulation of explanatory theories that tie these empirical observations together. Theory-building has always been a risky business in science—a theory, no matter how well it explains a multitude of observations, can be brought into question or even shot down entirely by a single contradictory observation or experiment. Theorists are a tiny minority in science; they must face a virtual army of experimentalists, each eager to be the first to disprove a theory with some cleverly–designed observation. Fortunately, an even larger army of experimentalists spend their lifetimes generating multitudes of new, esoteric, yet reliable observations. These observations are the grist for the mills of the undaunted theorists, who must, somehow, weld them together into a larger scientific whole.

What constitutes a good theory? William of Occam, a fourteenth-century British philosopher, suggested that, other things being equal, the best theory was the simplest theory. Science has generally adopted this mandate as "Occam's razor." Furthermore, theories, even if existing observations don't contradict them, are considered in poor taste if they cannot, at least in principle, be empirically verified or rejected. Also in poor taste are after-the-fact adjustments of theories to fit new empirical data, especially if these adjustments appear contrived, i.e., *ad hoc* in nature. A good theory not only explains the facts that its creator intended, but it suggests fresh possibilities that might be confirmed by newly devised experiments.

Science as an evolutionary process

Why are we humans able to scientifically comprehend nature? It's downright amazing that an animal has evolved the ability to grasp the essence of its own evolution, not to mention that of the entire universe. Of course, the goal of life from its inception has been the accumulation of information useful for its own survival and propagation. As noted by the late philosopher of science, Karl Popper, "From amoeba to Einstein, the growth of knowledge is always the same: we try to solve our problems and to obtain, by a process of elimination, something approaching adequacy in our tentative solutions." Modern science is an extremely powerful evolutionary process for generating, gathering, and organizing reliable information; we shouldn't be surprised that in a mere four hundred years it has made astonishing progress towards a comprehensive understanding of humanity and the cosmos.

Science is an evolutionary process similar in some ways to genetic evolution. Instead of genes, observations and theories compete. Instead of nature selecting which genes will survive, scientists select which observations and theories will survive. As with biological organisms and their amazingly evolved fit to the environment, science has evolved as a bridge between theories and the universe they attempt to explain. Unlike biological evolution, which leads to increasing diversity, science evolves toward increasing unity, a progressive trend resulting from the scientist's goal of devising a single universal explanation that will fit all of the pieces of the cosmic jigsaw puzzle together into one seamless picture.

In contrast to biological evolution, which at least for large animals proceeds at a glacial pace, science, a form of cultural evolution, has evolved with lightning speed. Protocol requires scientists to reduce theories to internationally understandable written descriptions—often including mathematical notation—and to publish them in refereed journals available to the public at large. The first to publish—not the first to discover—receives the credit. Such publications subject new observations or theories to the scrutiny of specialists worldwide, making them available to all for verification and further elaboration. This strong, first-to-publish selection pressure has hastened science's progress towards explaining reality. And it is the explanation of reality that is science's ultimate goal. As Paul Gross and Norman Levitt write:

> Reality is the overseer at one's shoulder, ready to rap one's knuckles or to spring the trap into which one has

> been led by overconfidence, or by a too-complacent reliance on mere surmise. Science succeeds precisely because it has accepted a bargain in which even the boldest imagination stands hostage to reality. Reality is the unrelenting angel with whom scientists have agreed to wrestle.

The depth of time

How did scientists discover who we are and how we came to be? They faced the same difficulty as their religious predecessors, having no concept whatsoever of the immense depth of time that stretched billions of years into the past, with few clues as to the many forms of life that preceded current life. Nevertheless, biologists set out with scientific zeal to impose order on life's prodigious variety. They grouped known plants and animals together based on a system for classifying and naming life forms devised by the Swedish naturalist Carolus Linneaus. If it looked like a duck and quacked like a duck, it was labeled a duck. Morphological classification in action. So began the planet-wide search for previously undescribed and unclassified life. As European ships and explorers spread around the planet, expedition naturalists shipped back well-preserved specimens of the exotic plants and animals they encountered to avid stay-at-home collectors.

From an anatomical point of view, it soon became clear with which other animals we humans should be classified. In 1699, Edward Tyson dissected a chimpanzee shipped from Angola to London, and orangutans and other apes soon appeared in European zoos and on the dissecting tables of European anatomists. However, the obvious physical similarities of apes to humans still gave us no reason to suspect our actual descent from apes. The entire notion of such descent made little sense in a world believed by many to be just six thousand years old. Zoo mates we might be, but certainly not family!

Meanwhile, geologists began classifying rock formations in much the same way biologists had classified life—they looked for similarities. They noticed that closely matched layers of rock occurred at widely spread locations; some of these layers were even embedded with matching types of seashells. A few even had the same kinds of fossil bones, presumably from extinct animals that perished in the Great Flood mentioned in the Bible. Geologists also observed that series of layers, piled one on top another in specific orders, formed matching sequences in widely different areas. Although often jumbled and occasionally presented in reverse order, the layers did seem to have a pervasive and identifiable "master" sequence.

In the early nineteenth century, English geologist Charles Lyle suggested that geological strata were sedimentary layers deposited on ocean bottoms by the gradual process of continental erosion over immense periods of time. These sea floor layers, originally soft silt, had been compressed over eons into rock and then raised, in a yet unknown manner, into mountains, becoming occasionally rearranged in the process. This explained the jumble. By observing how fast sediments were currently being deposited and by noting the depth of past layers, one could roughly estimate the ages of the various layers in the master sequence. These estimates quickly led geologists to calculate how long the entire sequence had taken to form, giving them a hint as to the age of the Earth. Far from a comfortable six thousand years, geologists concluded that the Earth was at least a few billion years old, an immensity of time that boggled everyone's imagination. Humanity had received an unexpected and unwelcome shock, and it was about to be compounded.

The voyage of the Beagle

When the twenty-three-year-old English naturalist Charles Darwin obtained a copy, hot off the press, of Lyle's revolutionary *Principles of Geology*—for light reading during his round-the-world voyage of exploration on H.M.S. Beagle—the stage was set for an extraordinary discovery. Darwin served as both the ship's naturalist and an intellectual companion for its captain, Robert Fitzroy. Like the seagoing naturalists before him, Darwin's main job was to obtain and preserve specimens for shipment back to England.

Having just read Lyle's book, Darwin also became an intent observer of the never-before-described geological formations of South America. He wrote accurate descriptions and knowledgeable interpretations of South American geology which he posted back to England, much to the delight of his scientist friends. He also avidly collected fossil bones, shipping them back to England by the crate-full.

Before crossing the Pacific, the Beagle stopped at the Galapagos Archipelago, a small group of seven islands lying some seven hundred miles west of South America, but only a few miles from each other. What Darwin observed on the Galapagos didn't make sense to his orderly mind. Instead of the normal variety of birds he had just observed on the South American mainland, he saw only numerous kinds of rather similar finches. Besides filling the niches normally reserved for finches, these birds also occupied the parrots' niches and various other birds' niches. What was going on here?

Slightly different species of finches, some with longer beaks, some with shorter beaks, occupied these various bird niches. Why, Darwin wondered, would God have used just a few minor variations on one type of bird for so many different jobs? He later wrote, "One might fancy from an original paucity of birds in this archipelago, one species had been taken and modified for different ends." And then there was the strange matter of the iguanas. Besides occupying their usual lizardly niche, other slightly varied species of iguanas were eating plants normally eaten by ungulates. All most unusual!

On returning to England, Darwin spent a number of years describing the specimens in his huge collection, while farming entire sections of it out to specialists. He also wrote an adventure journal aptly titled *The Voyage of the Beagle,* which saw numerous reprints. A favorite of scientists and non-scientists alike, it remains excellent reading to this day.

As Darwin worked and wrote, he mulled over the mystery of the strange finches and iguanas of the Galapagos. The most obvious explanation was that all the varieties of finches had descended from some original pair or flock of finches that had arrived from the mainland, perhaps shortly after the geological formation of the islands. But how had they split into separate species, each adapted to a somewhat different niche?

Darwin, long a fancier and breeder of racing pigeons, knew about the naturally-occurring variety in the offspring of animals. He realized that, to some extent, such variety was heritable. The key to the mystery of the Galapagos finches came to him while reading an essay by Thomas Malthus that suggested that while human populations expanded geometrically, their food supplies expanded only arithmetically. Thus in the long run there was bound to be more people than food to feed them. Darwin realized that this must also be true with animals—with all life, in fact. In a stroke of true genius, it dawned on Darwin that for each generation, some would be "selected" to live and procreate, while others would die off without having produced offspring. Unlike domesticated animals, whose survival and reproductive fate was primarily determined by humans, nature herself would select among wild animals, automatically choosing from the variety available those most capable of surviving, finding mates, and reproducing.

Darwin surmised that the original finches and iguanas on the Galapagos had diversified into a growing variety of specialists through a process of proliferating offspring, heritable variety, and natural selection—each variety of finches slowly evolving to more efficiently utilize the resources available in its selected niche. Once having nailed down this explanation for the finches and iguanas on the Galapagos, Darwin extended his hypothesis to state that such diversification and selection took place in all forms of life.

The evolution of culture

Darwin argued his case with great skill and scientific objectivity in *The Origin of Species,* first published in 1859. Not wishing to needlessly inflame religious sensibilities by including humanity in his tome, he discussed only non-human animals. Other scientists were not so reticent, however, and the evolution of humanity, both physical and social, became a hotly debated topic virtually overnight. A century and a half later, this argument continues unabated, at least in the United States.

A few overly eager evolutionary enthusiasts were quick to suggest that we had evolved from some common ancestor with the apes, but had taken a different road than our primate cousins to reach the brilliant evolutionary summit of European-dominated civilization. With almost no hominid fossil evidence available (and with little understanding of or empathy for the few remaining hunter-gatherer cultures), those in a hurry to apply Darwin's evolutionary insight to humanity mistakenly suggested that the various existing human races were living representatives of mankind's evolutionary steps from apes to Western civilization. These early anthropologists and social historians didn't realize that the common ancestor of humans and apes had actually lived many millions of years in the past, while the common ancestor for all current human races preceded us by only a couple of hundred thousand years. Racial differences, supposedly indicative of the long evolutionary history of hominids were, in fact, only a few minor variations accrued since the recent origin of modern *Homo sapiens*.

This error in evolutionary interpretation—this mistake of drawing extensive conclusions with insufficient supporting data—had serious social consequences. It provided a pseudo-scientific rationalization for the supposedly more advanced races (white Europeans) to treat other races as less than human. From the mistreatment of the descendents of slaves in the southern United States to the Nazi gassing of millions of Jews during World War II, racists used this false notion of human evolution to justify the grossest of inhumanities. .

In the early decades of the twentieth century, evidence gathered by anthropologists such as Franz Boas suggested that so-called primitive societies were, in actuality, not simpler, merely different. Languages and social customs appeared to be equally complex across all human societies. Civilizations, though obviously technically more complex than hunter-gatherer societies, were very recent phenomena, clearly unrelated to human physical evolution.

Meanwhile, physical anthropologists had discovered an increasing number of rare, hominid fossils. As they pieced together the real story of human evolution, it became apparent that our common ancestor with the apes was millions of years in the past, while the current races of humanity had only recently diverged from each other. But the damage had already been done and, as a result, many social anthropologists declared—

with moral indignation, if not scientific justification—their independence from evolutionary and biological dictates. Human behavior is molded by human cultures, they stated, and human behavior and cultures can be whatever humans choose them to be. Evolutionary thinking about human behavior and social organization is not only futile, they suggested, but it breeds racism. Thus, we should strongly discourage evolutionary thinking when it comes to humanity.

Removing human behavioral and social evolution from the scientific agenda created a problem for physical anthropologists such as Louis Leakey, however. Physical anthropologists wanted to know why hominids had physically evolved in the way the fossil record indicated. They suspected that changes in behavior and social organization were key evolutionary forces. In what ways had the behavior of our common ancestor with the apes evolved to that of modern *Homo sapiens*? Leakey, as mentioned earlier, realized that we didn't really understand the behavior of our nearest relatives, the great apes, because we based our assessment of their limited behavioral capabilities on observations of captive animals in zoos or laboratories. Leakey surmised that ape behavior in its natural setting would be very different, perhaps even surprisingly human. Leakey's three observers—Jane Goodall, Diane Fossey, and Buruti Galdikas—revolutionized our understanding of ape behavior. Slowly but surely, it again became permissible within the science community to consider human behavior and social organization in evolutionary terms.

World history

History is an academic discipline so entirely human, so tilted to the present (just the last five thousand years or so), that it generally is not considered science at all. Many historians have concerned themselves, quite legitimately, with the short run; a purely descriptive approach has often satisfied them. But the world historians, who wished to cover the whole of humanity's civilized experience, probed beyond the short-term appearance of randomness in search of longer-term trends and regularities. World historians, like scientists, looked for patterns, for lawful behavior.

Spengler, Toynbee, Sorokin and other world historians writing in the early twentieth century saw a cyclic behavior in the rise and fall of civilizations. They discerned a repeating pattern, not a long-term trend. Recently, however, world historians such as David Christian, Alfred Crosby, J. R. McNeill, William McNeill, and Clive Ponting have placed human history into scientific, biological, and even ecological contexts. Their work has revealed a long-term trend that stands out over both the medium-term cycles of civilization and the short-term accidents of history. William McNeill, for instance, pictures the last ten thousand years as the evolutionary unfolding of the consequences of agriculture. Crosby's biological interests are clear from his statement, "I insist that that which enables human beings to stay alive and reproduce and that which dispatches us to our eternal reward is worthy of our attention." This new breed of world historians no longer views history as a series of accidents or repeating cycles of rise and fall, but as a natural evolutionary process whose major features proceed in a logical and scientifically explicable manner.

Pandora's Box

Now, almost a century and a half after Darwin's *Origin of Species* was published, the evolutionary view provides a unifying theme across all the major scientific disciplines that are concerned with explaining who we are and how we came to be. But scientific progress has also summoned forth other, darker forces.

As the predawn darkness of the New Mexico desert ended suddenly on July 16, 1945, Robert Oppenheimer, the nuclear physicist and leader of The Manhattan Project that had developed the atomic bomb quoted from the *Bhagavad-Gita*:

> If the radiance of a thousand suns
> were to burst into the sky
> that would be like
> the splendor of the mighty one.

Watching the fiery mushroom cloud rise above the now brilliantly illuminated desert, he found expression for his despair, again in the *Bhagavad-Gita*:

Now I am become Death
The destroyer of worlds.

Three weeks later, Hiroshima was incinerated in a blinding flash. Tens of thousands were instantly killed. The atomic bomb was based on the purest, most advanced of the sciences—physics. Further, the most respected of scientists, Albert Einstein, had called for the bomb's development. Looking back from the post-war vantage point of 1947, Oppenheimer wrote, "In some sort of crude sense which no vulgarity, no humor, no overstatement can quite extinguish, the physicists have known sin; and this is a knowledge which they cannot lose."

Francis Bacon's dream of a Golden Age of Science, of benefit to all humankind, had taken a bizarre turn. Scientists' curiosity had led them into areas of knowledge that humanity was ill-equipped to handle. Having pried open Pandora's Box, they seemed powerless to regulate what emerged. The forbidden knowledge they'd released was now loose in the world, and there was no way to stuff it back into the box or, for that matter, to even shut the lid against the escape of further evils.

The explosion of science

The Manhattan Project that developed the atomic bomb wasn't the only government effort that massively funded scientific research. World War II marks the beginning of government funding of science on a scale undreamt of prior to the war. The Cold War continued to fuel the era of "big science," an era of large, well-funded investigative teams that replaced lone scientists working on a shoestring.

Digital computers soon replaced human computers. Previously forced to primarily work with simplified, linear analytic solutions, powerful computers allowed scientists to tackle nonlinear problems and create highly complex models of naturalistic phenomena. As the power of computers grew, so did the sophistication of the computerized models of reality. Several generations of scientists have now been refining and expanding the computer models first coded in the 1950's. Hundreds of lines of codes have expanded to tens of thousands of lines. The close match between the computer models and observations had become extraordinary in many areas of science. Teams of scientists spend entire careers refining a computerized model

In parallel with the development of sophisticated computer models, scientists also started using computers to gather data. Although large mainframe computers were not adept at real-time data-gathering, PCs were ideally suited to the task. In every area of science, PCs rapidly replaced human observers and data recorders. Pen and ink were out; PCs and floppies were in. I was part of this revolution. My 1982 book, *Real-Time Control with the TRS-80,* explained how to use one of the earliest PCs to not only gather scientific data, but to automatically control observations. With my partner Louis Boyd, fully automatic PC-controlled astronomical observations were made in 1983, and we soon had a fully-automated mountaintop observatory in operation with multiple robotic telescopes. Space-qualified PCs soon became the brains of observatories in Earth orbit and spacecraft sent to explore the solar system.

Not only did government funding and computers greatly impact the conduct of science, so did the Internet—originally a government-funded innovation aimed at improving communication among university scientists engaged in research for the military. Rapid communication between scientists worldwide greatly speeded up the pace of scientific research. Soon vast quantities of data, most of it gathered by PCs, was transferred over the Internet. Boyd and I were among the first scientists to use the Internet to not only control remote observations, but to retrieve the resulting data—all automatically while astronomers got a good night's sleep.

The combination of government funding, computers, and the Internet have resulted in a virtual explosion of science since World War II. Crick and Watson's opening into the world of DNA has, in only a few decades (thanks very much to computers), led to sequencing of the entire human genome. Space telescopes have reached back to the beginning of the universe. The increase in human knowledge resulting from the explosion of science is almost incalculable.

The enigma of science

We are left, now, with the enigma of science. For four billion years, life on Earth never bothered to ask how it came to be. Then, becoming aware of its own mortality, it finally asked the question. Our socially evolved brains supplied humanly pleasing and spiritually creative answers. Then, just four hundred years ago, modern science began its successful search for empirical reality. Now we know the science story of how we came to be. We also know the answers to a few questions we wish that we had never asked. As we look to the future, we are grateful for the good life that science and technology have provided us; grateful to the machines that do our work. But we are wary, even fearful, of the creatures we have become, of the unintended consequences of our power and knowledge. Having eaten from science's tree of knowledge, we have truly left the Garden of Eden.

PART III

What is our Fate?
Four alternative finales

Any effort to foretell the course of politics,
of social relations, of religious beliefs,
or even of science itself over the next century
is pure arrogance.

Robert Heilbroner

If seed in the black earth can turn into such beautiful roses,
what might not the heart of man become in its long journey
towards the stars.

G. K. Chesterton

Chapter 9

CHIMPANZEE PARADISE
High-tech Garden of Eden

One of the great dreams of man must be to find
some place between the extremes of nature and civilization
where it is possible to live without regret.
Barry Lopez

Are not the mountains, waves, and skies a part
Of me and of my soul, as I of them?
George Gordon, Lord Byron

Alternative futures—an introduction

What is our fate? Since science has provided an objective, extensive, and reliable explanation for how we came to be, we can be excused for thinking that science should be able to forecast our fate and inform us of ways we could influence it. After all, science is predicting the fate of the universe and has a solid understanding of how four billion years of evolution has produced millions of diverse species on this planet. One would hope that science could forecast where a single species is headed on one tiny little planet orbiting a run-of-the-mill star. Sadly, such a forecast appears to beyond the capabilities of science.

Science is good at making long-term predictions for simple systems when the forces are few or historical precedents are numerous. It has difficulty, however, reliably predicting complex, one-time situations influenced by many parameters, some of which appear to be random. It may be impossible, even in theory, to make such predictions. Small initial effects can send complex systems off in entirely unpredictable directions ala the famed Butterfly Effect.

Short-term predictions are a wholly different ball game. Governments and businesses pay a growing number of futurists serious money to make short-term forecasts, typically just five, ten, or at the most twenty years into the future. While not always right, these forecasts are accurate enough to be useful as planning aids. What these futurists do best is extrapolate current trends in an objective, often mathematical manner. Many of these short-term predictions are of a contingent nature—if certain circumstance X comes to pass, then it follows, with some degree of probability, that consequence Y will be the outcome. Such contingent predictions can be helpful guides for choosing between alternative courses of action.

With respect to the fate of humanity, however, our primary interest isn't in the distant future, millions or billions of years from now. On the other hand, the futurist's modest projections of current trends a decade or two into the future isn't what we're looking for either. Our main concern is the probable outcome of the impending collision between an aggressively expanding humanity and a finite planet. This is the prediction we would like to have—the prediction of humanity's fate.

Although predicting humanity's fate is beyond science, we can take a page from the futurists' book and consider several alternatives. By changing various key assumptions, we can consider how these changes might lead to starkly different futures. Scientists, for instance, disagree over how robust our planet's ecosystem might be. A few scientists think it's like a highly interconnected house of cards; our carelessness could easily bring it tumbling down. Other scientists contend that living associations are only loosely connected, and mere humans are not about to cause the planet's ecosystem to collapse. Some scientists argue that humanity has a modicum of control over its own destiny; others feel this is wishful thinking—we aren't in control now, never have been, and never will be.

The many differing views within science can generate a virtual infinity of possible futures. What follows are four alternative futures that represent a sample from these wide-ranging possibilities. Developed to stress differences, these alternatives sharply and purposely disagree with one another. Each future champions its own case while, at the same time, disparaging the other possibilities for the future. Readers can decide for themselves which alternative is most likely or, for that matter, which is most desirable. We turn first to *Chimpanzee Paradise: High-tech Garden of Eden.*

Healthy living

If humanity is truly capable of self-restraint—admittedly this is a considerable assumption—why not do it right? Why not go all out and fully restrain ourselves? Although self-restraint could unlock the door to a virtual infinity of "unnatural" futures, let us consider a self-control so complete that we created a true paradise on Earth, a virtual Garden of Eden.

Our bodies and minds have evolved over millions of years to serve lives spent in small groups hunting and gathering on the plains of Africa. Natural selection hasn't yet had time to revise our bodies or rewire our brains for civilized life, for conditions radically different from those prevailing in prehistoric Africa. We should strive to create an environment in which humans will be physically, mentally, and even socially healthy.

Throughout civilization's long history, the most common diet problem has been under consumption, the most common physical problem—over work. Our modern era, driven by fossil-fuel machines, has produced huge food surpluses for many, and freed much of humanity from agricultural labor. The most pressing health problems in industrialized nations today are over-consumption and under-exercise—problems formerly restricted to the elite. Fat, sugar, and salt, which were all rare and difficult-to-obtain commodities in our hunter-gatherer past, have now become abundant.

Through science, we're learning what's conducive to human health and what's detrimental, both physically and psychologically. We're learning that the lifestyle to which humans became genetically adapted over the ages is generally a healthy one. Conversely, practices that are novel and new, that we haven't had time to genetically adapt to, are often unhealthy. Exceptions exist, of course, in both directions. Studying and understanding the healthy aspects of the hunter-gatherer lifestyle doesn't imply returning to it; we can reap its benefits in our own, modern way. Our ancestors did not have the luxury of antibiotics, tetanus shots, anesthetics, plaster casts, glasses, false teeth, or pyramid guides to the four food groups.

It is clear, however, that humans need four of the hunter-gatherer virtues: a varied diet, frequent physical exercise, variety in daily experience, and a sense of personal involvement that comes from belonging to a small group of family and friends that we increasingly value over the years. Social animals, we need our mates, children, relatives, and friends; we even need our pets and, perhaps, our mothers-in-law. We require intimate, long-lasting relationships. We are lost without community. We do best when changes are slow-paced, when grandparents and grandchildren don't live in radically different worlds. We gather psychic strength from a close and harmonious coexistence with nature. We look back with nostalgia to the Garden of Eden, for we've never forgotten our true home.

A healthy, sustainable future does not necessarily imply a non-technical future. In fact, if we are to regain Eden, it would be disastrous for us to abandon science or technology at this crucial juncture. Science can suggest how we could heal the Earth's ecosystems, and we need new technologies such as solar power to make our presence ecologically benign. Of course, more of the wrong sorts of science and technology, such as nuclear weapons, could be disastrous, but so could an insufficient dose of the right sorts. We must depend on science, our most reliable source of information, to convince humanity of its peril and the nature of its salvation.

Returning to Eden

Until recently it would have been difficult for culturally diverse humanity to agree on much of anything. Science now provides us with a unified, cross-cultural view of humanity, of the world, of who we are, of how we came to be, and of our alternatives for the future. The last few crucial pieces of science's evolutionary view of humanity have only recently clicked into place. We didn't even understand the basic nature of life until James Watson and Francis Crick discovered the structure of DNA in 1953. It was in the 1960s that Jane Goodall began her observations of chimpanzees in the wild. Only since the 1980s and 1990s have the natural and social sciences began their unification through a common evolutionary view of Earth and humanity.

Unification of purpose and direction is now within humanity's grasp. Individuals everywhere can now understand the human situation from a unified biological and ecological perspective. Spreading wide the basic understanding of humanity and the planet provided by our scientific, evolutionary views, we could cause changes in corporate, governmental, and military policies, making them more supportive of the health of both humanity and the Earth. *Homo sapiens* can no longer consider itself apart from the rest of life on this planet. McDonalds and Exxon, not to mention Walmart, could serve the common good rather than their major stockholders.

As the new millennium gets under way, an increasing number of people are expressing environmental concerns. While this demonstrates that their hearts are in the right place, most measures are still cosmetic compared with the colossal scale of the problems. Though the conservation movement has raised public awareness and won a few small victories, a tidal wave of destruction continues to wash over us. As more humans learn of our true ecological situation, however, perhaps our combined efforts can effectively channel the course of cultural evolution in a more desirable direction. Our most important action of all may be to educate the public as to the nature of our present circumstances and our future prospects.

Our closest relatives, the chimpanzees and bonobos, as well as the other great apes, the gorillas and orangutans, are all headed toward extinction as the last of the great equatorial jungles are chain-sawed and bulldozed to oblivion. This should give us pause. Will we be next? The present diversity of life took sixty-five million years to build up after a mega-meteor struck the Earth. If nothing halts the present human-perpetuated mass extinction, the diversity of life will plummet yet again. It would take millions of years to recover.

Having promoted ourselves to be Masters of the Earth, we owe it to other life and to the planet itself to take charge of that rogue ape, humanity, and preserve what biological diversity still remains. We need to switch from being the planet's chief plunderer to being its primary guardian.

One might think it would be best if humanity were to reintegrate itself into natural ecosystems as quickly as possible. But with our present billions, such an act would devastate what little non-human life remains. We must do exactly the opposite; we must separate humanity from the remaining natural ecosystems. We need to quarantine this dangerous species and its domestic side-kicks from all others. We are different from all other life—truly unique—and will remain so. The human cultural genie cannot be stuffed back into nature's genetic bottle. Our presence will forevermore require control. Having eaten the fruit from the Tree of Knowledge, we can't return to the Garden of Eden without careful self-supervision.

As we reduce our numbers, we may increasingly be able to enjoy a rejuvenated Eden, but we can never return to it as innocent Adams and Eves. Even if we actually could leave our science and technology behind, without careful monitoring the blitzkrieg would only occur once again. Humanity must become and remain a carefully organized and controlled planetary superorganism that watches over the Earth—and itself—with intelligent foresight and constant vigilance.

The Guardians

From our current vantage point, it is difficult to envision a future in which there are only millions instead of billions of humans, a future in which the pace of progress itself has slowed to a crawl. Throughout most human history, however, the social changes from one generation to the next were usually imperceptible. Progress, until recently, was a foreign concept. If we thought about it at all, we perceived the past as better than the present.

The idea of progress as being good, even inevitable, is a modern suggestion that was initiated by the likes of Francis Bacon and Adam Smith. It reached its Victorian peak prior to World War I. With atomic bombs, ozone holes, and a clearly overcrowded planet, we now view progress, at best, as a two-edged sword. Could progress have ever been more than a transient phase? Science, after all, can only make rapid progress as long as there are major discoveries left to be made. While important discoveries certainly remain, they are already fewer and farther in between. Capitalism, which prospers from science, technical progress, and expansion, must also eventually subside; infinite expansion is simply impossible. From a vantage point far in the future, the era of major scientific discoveries, rampant technology, and unbridled capitalism will be remembered as a fleeting phase of sudden, unusual change, just as Big Macs will fade from our memory.

The great gift of this transitory phase will be a universal age of plenty. Before the transition, only the elite of civilization led the good life, but after it—thanks to the hard-working, productive, robotic machines and bountiful new sources of clean energy—all humans (the optimum few hundred million that remain in the new era) will delight in universal wealth. Breakfast at Tiffany's for all.

We might view the entire past ten thousand years of agriculture, civilization, and science as a short, labor-intensive, turbulent phase between two well-adapted, leisurely eras. We humans like to do what we're naturally fit to do, what we evolved for millions of years to do, and that doesn't include hard work in the hot sun or monotonous toil in factories or offices. Once burned, twice shy. We are chimpanzees, not ants!

Freed from the necessity for work, from the anxiety of constant change, from economic insecurity, we'll do what humanity has always done under such circumstances: relax and enjoy ourselves. In fact, Gunther Stent, in his *The Coming of the Golden Age*, suggested that we had already set out on this path in the 1960s. The hippies and beatniks pointed the way for the rest of humanity. Music, sex, and peace will be in. Work, competition, and war will be out. The peaceful, social, laid-back bonobos should become our role models

Without the fear that new scientific revelations will constantly blindside us, our myths and religions of all sorts will prosper as never before in an explosion of human creativity. Our imaginations have always exceeded mere objective reality. Science's theories, such as the theory of evolution, will soon be about as exciting as the revelation that the Earth is round, not flat. As religions take scientific fact as an obvious, boring given, those things which have always intrigued humanity—our imaginative stories, speculative new ideas, creative art and music—will flower in a profusion of cultural diversity.

Far from lacking challenge and a life mission, the citizens of the New Golden Age will have their hands full acting as the overseers and caretakers of an entire planet. They will be occupied for many centuries restoring the planet from the ravages of the transitional phase, not to mention maintaining human population at its optimal level.

As guardians of the planet, we will, presumably, defend the Earth against planet-busting meteors. Most of all, however, we'll defend the planet against ourselves. We'll insist on becoming and remaining responsible citizens of planet Earth. To this end, we'll apply our newly unified scientific understanding of life and humanity, how we came to dominate the planet, and how we avoided disaster at the last minute by taking firm charge of ourselves and our only home. For this understanding, we owe a great debt to the environmentalists who have led the charge. Lest we slip back into our old, irresponsible ways, we must forevermore inoculate our young by teaching them the cautionary story of the chimpanzees who would be ants.

Chapter 10

BOOM AND BUST

May the punishment fit the crime

The end of the human race will be that
it will eventually die of civilization
Ralph Waldo Emerson

Competition is racing along in high gear,
but the train is running off the track.
Hubert Reeves

Easter Island, Earth Island

Chimpanzee paradise? A return to the Garden of Eden while retaining our high-tech capabilities? A nice, warm-fuzzy vision, but a totally unrealistic Pollyannish suggestion. There is no indication whatsoever that we're different from any other animals with respect to self control. Species self-restraint would be unnatural, entirely against our evolutionary grain. Every species expands its numbers, given the opportunity. Unrestrained, species explode until they hit resource or pollution limits, and then they crash—even faster than they expanded. This is evolution's way.

Easter Island is the preview of coming attractions. Polynesians, arriving on this small, forested island paradise, rapidly increased in numbers. Adding insult to the injury of the small island, two religious groups competed with each other to place the most stone statues on the coast looking out to sea. Moving the massive statues from the quarries to the coast required rollers, and the Polynesians cut down the forests to provide the roller logs. In time, the last tree was felled, the land eroded, the population crashed, and their civilization was lost. When Europeans came across the island some years later, its few remaining inhabitants, barely scratching out a living, had no idea of the heights they had once achieved.

Is Earth island headed for a crash?

Since 1950, consumption of seafood has expanded by a factor of four, as has our consumption of fossil fuels. In the single decade from 1985-1995, the WorldWatch Institute estimates that the planet's economy expanded by $4 trillion, more than the total economic expansion of all civilizations from the Sumerians to 1950.

The combination of increased agricultural yield and reduced death rates over the past century has created an explosion of human population. Humanity has been doubling its numbers every forty years for centuries, a rate that simply can't continue since we're already using 40 percent of the primary productivity of the planet. That is, 40 percent of both wild and domesticated vegetation—the primary producers on this planet—are already used by humans in one way or another.

Although big game hunting, and then agriculture, resulted in significant population growth, it was the combination of machines and science that supported our sudden increase in numbers, our final burst of growth. Technology's gift of machines cleared and leveled the land, pumped water, and transported food around the planet. Science's gifts of sanitation, antibiotics, immunizations, and insecticides prolonged human life cheaply and effectively. With these factors in mind, it's hardly surprising that we have begun to encounter planetary limits. According, again, to the WorldWatch Institute, grain land area peaked in 1981 when land lost to salination, desertification, and urbanization exceeded new land brought into grain cultivation. Planet-wide use of fertilizers peaked in 1989 because increased use would not have resulted in any increased productivity. Total grain production peaked in the following year, 1990, along with the amount of usable irrigation water. Our species, *Homo sapiens*, after less than two hundred thousand years of population expansion, is quickly becoming too big for its planetary britches.

We are consuming resources faster than nature, or even we ourselves, can replace them. We started down this path over 10,000 years ago as well-organized big game hunters.

Soon much of the big game was gone, followed by the smaller game. Wild fruits and vegetables disappeared next. As agriculture expanded and more land was put to the plow or grazed, increasing portions of agricultural land were lost forever to soil erosion, salination, and desertification. All these processes began with Sumer and other early civilizations. Now there are no new continents, no new fertile places to farm. Food production has peaked and is headed downward, while the Earth's human population continues to soar, albeit at a somewhat slower rate than earlier predicted. With the entire planet harnessed to feed a single species, it appears that we're about to run short of food and water. Our moment of truth approaches. Thus, our second possible future: boom and bust.

Complexity adjustments and overshoots

For simple societies, increases in complexity can often be beneficial. We saw earlier that complex insect societies, the insect superorganisms, pushed solitary insects to the periphery of their colonies, leaving them just a few crumbs, so to speak. We have also discussed how civilizations have relegated less complex societies, those of the hunter-gatherers, to remote corners of the world with an even more meager allotment of crumbs.

But as complexity increases and societies grow ever more populous, reciprocal payoffs eventually diminish. The easy pickings, the low-hanging fruit, are gleaned first, making further gains increasingly difficult. At some point, the advantages of additional complexity or larger organizational scale are offset by the shrinking size of the agricultural and industrial returns. The growth of complexity does not stop at this optimal point, however. Nature never redesigns things from scratch; it tacks improvements onto existing structures. Civilizations are no different. They solve new problems by applying more specialists, another layer of bureaucracy, or some novel technical fix. As the number of problems civilizations encounter has no end, neither does their mindless accumulation of complexity—at least not until it is too late.

Many civilizations have gone bust in the past. Overly complex or populous civilizations crashed, adjusting to create simpler, more efficient societies with smaller, i.e., more sustainable populations. Analogously, we might expect the present global, interconnected, highly complex, and carefully integrated international system that supports over six billion humans to crash and be replaced with a less integrated system that supports fewer people. Complex societies have always been difficult to maintain, vulnerable to problems of their own making, and prone to collapse. By considering the failings of earlier societies, we can make reasonable projections about the impending collapse of our own.

Historic booms and busts

Ant superorganisms are fortunate in that other life has always restrained their growth (though they might not consider this a boon if they were actually capable of thinking about it). Checks and balances co-evolved with the ants while they were leisurely exploring the possibilities of the superorganism realm. Ants should thank other life for restraining them and thus enabling them to be sustainable and successful over the long haul. In their heart of hearts, ants share our greed for expansion, but other life fortuitously saved them from themselves.

Human superorganisms have been less fortunate. Without effective checks from other life, they have often zoomed right past their points of optimality into rapidly diminishing returns. Like earthquakes, we have, time and again, built up complexity tensions and then released them all at once in a spasmodic adjustment back to simpler societies that were mere vestiges of their grander pasts.

Rome is the classic example. Initially, the Roman Empire, with modest investment in its military and transport, brought in immense surpluses from all the shores and ports of the Mediterranean. In this way, Rome reaped an outstanding return on a small investment. As time passed, however, the empire became ever more bureaucratic, taxes rose, and standing garrisons grew ever larger. In the increasingly disgruntled provinces, the elite earned more for doing less, and the oppressed, home-front masses had to be bribed into submission with ever-larger doles and bloodier circuses. Eventually, the empire's capacity to respond to new problems was exhausted and Rome collapsed.

The Maya are another textbook example of unchecked expansion. As surpluses and complexity grew, competition increased between the Maya city-states. An arms race among them spiraled out of control. No city-state dared opt out of the race; if it had, a neighbor would have instantly grabbed it. The fragile jungle environment was eventually exhausted. The city-states, locked in mortal combat, collapsed together, and life reverted to a simpler, pre-civilized state, as the jungles reclaimed the once-proud monuments.

Signs of diminishing returns

Our situation today, while broadly similar to these true stories of doom, is unique in several ways. Unlike earlier times, the world today teems with complex societies. It's somewhat like the Maya dilemma, in that each expression of the human superorganism is entangled with the rest, but on a much grander scale. As a result, collapse—when it comes—will be global, not local.

It is in the interest of the major global powers that the current world system does not collapse in a cultural earthquake that devastates them all. As the industrial countries still have considerable reserve wealth, it seems likely that they will be able to carry on for quite some time. However, the longer collapse is avoided, the more spectacular it may be when it comes. But are we really headed towards a collapse?

Everywhere, we can see the evidence of diminishing returns; the signs of runaway consumption are marked. Every year, we lose more farmland than we gain by clearing the last forests on the planet. Food production in the most populous country, China, peaked in 1990, while its population continues to grow. Despite heroic efforts, China's food supply just can't keep pace. The result, almost certainly, will be its increased reliance on imports and an increased scarcity (and price) of basic food commodities worldwide.

The production of oil, the energy from which the current high yields of agriculture stem and with which we redistribute vast quantities of food about the planet, will soon peak. We're now depleting oil fields faster than we can find replacements. Other vital minerals are following this same downward curve.

As lower-quality ores are tapped, they consume ever greater amounts of energy for their refining, leaving larger mounds of waste behind.

These obvious signs of a complex, worldwide social system headed for collapse have not been lost on a well-informed citizenry. People—especially in the rich, complex societies—are concerned with the pending breakdown of society, and some societal segments are already searching for ways to extricate themselves from this creeping complexity and the attendant collapse. A grow-your-own, make-your-own sort of lifestyle is gaining adherents.

Even more extreme are the growing number of survivalists who, certain of civilization's doom, are stocking up on life's basic necessities, including food, water, and ammunition. They train themselves in the use of weapons and military tactics which they will surely need to defend their hoarded supplies. They are apparently oblivious to the fact that much of the world's population would be delighted to simply know the source of their next meal, never mind worrying about filling a room with future sustenance.

The crash as a readjustment

We might consider the collapse, when it comes, as a normal, even expected, readjustment to a less complex, less populous, more efficient way of life—a corrective adjustment, if you will. Perhaps we should welcome this fate—the sooner it happens, the less severe it will be. The longer we stave off this necessary adjustment, the greater the resource consumption and waste production that will be required to support an increasingly inefficient and larger international society. The longer we put off the crash, the more the planet will bear the scars of civilization. With cold-hearted logic, we should conclude that we should take our medicine now rather than later.

From the viewpoint of the few hunter-gatherers still hanging on in the Amazon rain forest, a quick, clean global collapse of the industrial economies could be a blessing. With gasoline and diesel fuel unavailable, the chain saws and bulldozers threatening their forest homes would fall silent. With no ships to transport wood veneers and beef to the industrialized countries, the invasion of the Amazon would grind to a halt.

For those living in large cities, however, a global collapse would spell unmitigated disaster. Urbanites have become dependent on food grown elsewhere, often halfway around the planet—food that requires a high level of organization and energy for its growth, transport, processing, and distribution. If a global collapse disrupts oil supplies, or if oil supplies become scarce and hence expensive, then the current world population— let alone an even larger population—would not be supportable. Mass starvation and brutal conflict over the scraps would soon take us down to a more sustainable level—a level locally supportable without fossil-fuel machines. Without appropriately distributed oil and functioning fossil-fuel machines, the world's sustainable population is probably a billion or less. A sudden collapse could reduce it even further. While many millions would remain alive after the collapse, most of Earth's billions would perish.

Not just another bust?

But would this be the end of civilization? Could the survivors, sadder but wiser, pick up the pieces and move on, perhaps merely to boom and bust over and over again as other animal species have done? The coming bust may well be much more than an adjustment of social complexity and population. Perhaps it will be a permanent change, one brought on by the irreversible effects of agriculture, machines, and science. What if, rather than driving around the block again in yet another cycle of boom and bust, we're headed down a one-way street? It may be a dead end for civilization or even for humanity itself.

From a biological perspective, the human superorganisms we call civilizations are Johnny-come-latelies, mere infants. Human superorganisms have already achieved biological noteworthiness, thanks to the spectacular increase of their individual members from five million to five billion in only ten thousand years. This rapid growth has given human superorganisms a biomass equivalent to that of the eight thousand species of ants combined, and we achieved it by evolving culturally instead of genetically. We are an evolutionary experiment never before attempted—at least on this planet.

Our experiment has been spectacularly successful so far—if one equates success with biomass. However the very speed and magnitude of our growth raises biological red flags suggesting that human civilizations have proliferated without effective restraint by other life. If our emerging planetary superorganism follows the usual biological cycle of unrestrained growth, there's no question as to the outcome: nature itself will eventually restrain us. Resource scarcity, self-pollution, or restraint by other life will bring a sudden halt to the geometric expansion of human flesh. There is, biologically speaking, nothing unusual about this scenario—life is forever slipping past normal restraints, even if only locally and temporarily. The booms are almost always followed by even faster busts. We should presume that human superorganisms will follow this biological cycle on a planetary scale.

Algae in cold-weather ponds bloom every spring right after the spring thaw. Due to their rapid multiplication, the algae soon consume all the nutrients that have accumulated over the winter and their population crashes. During the next winter, the nutrients replenish themselves, and the cycle repeats itself. In our case, the planet is the pond. If we suddenly exhaust the planet's nutrients, however, it could be millions of years before they're able to regenerate.

The dead-end nature of evolution

The evolutionary fate of most lineages is dead-end extinction. Species of large mammals typically last about four million years. A few of them continue on by way of daughter species, but most terminate without issue, leaving the evolutionary tree a tangle of dead-end branches and twigs. Although mass extinctions occasionally exterminate species in wholesale lots, the end for most species is lonelier. Evolution has an unkind and amoral penchant for mindlessly promoting the immediately useful without concern for the long haul. Most species follow this shortsighted approach, taking advantage of some new opportunity, some temporary surplus in one of the planet's many ecological pathways. Once they have genetically modified themselves to milk this new opportunity for all it's worth, the transient opportunity usually goes away, leaving the unfortunate species high and dry with a now worthless, specialized, and usually fatal adaptation. That's the way of life. Thanks, evolution.

Cultural evolution, as is certainly the case for genetic evolution, promotes practices that are immediately useful, even if they're harmful, even fatal, in the long run. Consider agriculture: farming does allow a larger number of humans to be supported in the short run. But if farming always and necessarily causes irreversible and increasing damage to the planet's ecosystem in the long run, the ecosystem will, in the end, be able to support even fewer humans. Agriculture could always be a dead end.

Energy consumption could also be our downfall, as more complex systems require greater energy to maintain. Modern civilizations, with their fossil fuel machines, are extremely energy intensive. Our nearly total reliance on irreplaceable fossil fuels may represent another dead-end approach to life.

We are not in control

Would humanity ever allow itself to proceed down a one-way path to extinction? Many scientists believe that we may indeed allow exactly that, the primary reason being that humans really aren't in control. Since the first city-states of Sumer, human superorganisms have been competing both militarily and economically. The best-organized and most efficient human superorganisms have survived and prospered at the expense of the less efficient. Starting a thousand years ago, the highly competitive and aggressive countries of Western Europe developed capitalism, which has now spread planet-wide. Economic efficiency is now the evolutionary force controlling humanity. Like biological evolutionary forces, short-term economic efficiency is blind to the future and lives for the present.

But aren't we taking control by becoming environmentally conscious? Or are our efforts to stem the rapid rise in human population, consumption, and environmental impact so small—compared to the tidal wave of humanity and its machines—as to be insignificant? If so, are conservation movements to date just palliatives thrown up by so-called democracies, while the global corporations, which are in real control, continue to vie with each other for the planet's rapidly dwindling resources? These giants have little regard for protecting the environment, let alone reducing resource consumption. Even where laws against pollution have been passed, corporations continue to pollute on a massive scale, preferring to pay the minuscule fines imposed on them or, alternately, move their operations to countries with lax environmental laws more to their liking. The impact of conservation measures on the poorest countries, where the greatest increases in human population and environmental destruction are taking place, is essentially nil. In these countries, the scramble is on to clear the last forests, to raise a bit of food, and to burn the last wood to cook the food.

It's fashionable to believe that our current difficulties are the result of some spiritual deficiency, a defect in our Western psyche. If we could somehow correct this defect and convert the masses to peace-loving, Eastern-thinking, green-friendly environmentalists, we could avoid humanity's impending collision with our planetary limits. But several decades of environmental preaching have had little effect. Industrialized countries, where consumption has skyrocketed, remain wedded to their shopping malls and to the "good" life. Life has always strived to maximize its numbers, to grab the largest share of resources possible. Why should we expect it to change now? We are just doing what comes naturally, doing what evolution has, for almost four billion years, fine-tuned and firmly ingrained into all life on this planet.

The final crash

We speed ever on, even accelerate towards our doom. Although we are increasingly aware of our fate, our realization comes too late to gain control, even if we really tried. The inertia of humanity and of the environment itself will enable our full speed, head-long rush into the brick wall of planetary finiteness. We will still have our foot on the gas when we crash full force. Like a slow-motion nightmare, we'll be aware of what's happening but powerless to stop it. It's difficult to predict exactly how the end will come, so we must content ourselves with a few possibilities.

The scale of industrial activities has become threatening. According, yet again, to the WorldWatch Institute, industrial flows of nitrogen and sulfur are now both larger than natural flows. Human-induced circulations of cadmium, zinc, arsenic, mercury, nickel, and vanadium are twice that of natural flows. What if we inadvertently switch the geophysical state of the Earth into some new, unfavorable mode? Our carbon dioxide emissions could cause a runaway greenhouse effect, melting icecaps, flooding low-lying land, and drastically altering climate. Or, on the other hand, they might trigger the next ice age.

A nuclear war seems less likely now than it did a couple of decades ago, but what will happen when we run seriously short of oil? The fight over the last oil could easily escalate into nuclear warfare.

Nor should we lightly dismiss the possibility of an infectious disease wiping out humanity. The Black Death killed a third of humankind. The flu pandemic of 1917 killed twenty million. Our indiscriminate use of antibiotics has carelessly moved the agents of major afflictions well along their evolutionary pathways toward total antibiotic resistance. Much of this indiscriminate use has been in the name of minor increases in big corporation agricultural efficiency. The combined biomass of humanity is the largest, one-species edible jackpot on the planet, and astronomical hordes of microbes are busily working to see which can be the first to find the winning combination to the biggest payoff ever. It's only a matter of time.

Most threatening of all, however, may be the usual plows and chainsaws. When all the forests are gone, when all of the arable land is intensively farmed, and when the human population doubles yet again, the planet's ecosystems could be permanently, irreversibly damaged. Easter Island, Earth Island. A planet devoted entirely to humans and their domesticated plants, animals, and machines may simply not be viable.

If our bust proves sufficiently severe and abrupt, humanity might even become extinct, taking many other species down with us in the final catastrophe. Life on Earth has undergone mass extinction at least five times in the past, and it's becoming clear that the planet is now well into its sixth mass extinction. All the previous mass extinctions have been due to a loss of habitat. In those previous extinctions, this loss came in the form of abrupt climatic changes—very abrupt, in the case of the meteor that struck the Yucatan peninsula sixty-five million years ago, unleashing an explosive force ten thousand times as great as all of humanity's nuclear weapons combined. A different kind of comet struck Earth a few thousand years ago—civilized humanity. Having been responsible for the devastation of the planet, there might be some justice in our extinction, our complete and total demise. May the punishment fit the crime!

Chapter 11

PLANETARY SUPERORGANISM
All together on the global farm

We have become, by the power of a glorious
revolutionary accident called intelligence,
the steward of life's continuity on earth.
We did not ask for this role, but we cannot abjure it.
We may not be suited to it, but here we are.
Stephen Jay Gould

Ahead of us lies the potential to build a great civilization
in which our role in the world is a positive one,
managing sustainable resources and
enhancing the quality of our environment.
Daniel B. Botkin

Out to lunch

Gloom and doom. The Old Testament prophets told us that the world's imminent demise was just around the corner. Thomas Malthus gave scientific weight to this tradition when he described how Britain's population was increasing geometrically while its food supply was increasing only arithmetically; his conclusion? Massive starvation would soon set things right. Although Malthus' conjecture inspired Darwin's theory of evolution, its forecast for Britain's imminent demise was wrong. New resources increased even faster than the population. The result, rather than being a crash, was increasing prosperity, a virtual golden age.

A few decades ago, scientists—ecologists this time—became concerned that we might soon crash. Political environmentalists were delighted to have the scientific support of ecologists in their fight to save the planet. On studying the matter further, however, the flip-flop ecologists concluded that nature, by way of massive volcanic eruptions, extensive droughts, widespread fires, and severe ice ages, had already been more disruptive than humanity could ever dream of being. Nor, they informed the turn-back-the-clock environmentalists, did there appear to be any single "natural state" to which we could return. Ecosystems were constantly changing, sometimes with considerable speed. Furthermore, the ecologists' renounced their earlier view of a delicate, interlocking ecosystem that could easily collapse and replaced it with a new view that ecological associations in nature were robust. A crash no longer appeared likely. Scientists are so fickle!

What were environmentalists to do? They had lost the heart of their scientific rationale. Not to worry—a few scientists still supported them. There was still some small chance that humankind might cause a collapse. Besides, they'd already converted the younger generation. It had become a tenet of environmental faith that we were headed straight for the brick wall, that only a spiritual greening, an abandonment of our evil, consumptive lifestyles could save us. As in previous decades, however, there remained those rational minds (especially those who still had to work for a living) who continued to dismiss the perennial forecasts of gloom and doom as the coffee-house wailings of the idle offspring of the rich—existentialist crybabies one and all.

The real golden age

While it may appear that we are pushing up against planetary limits, in actuality we're only experiencing minor birthing pains as we transition from genetic to cultural planetary domination. We remain a long way from the carrying capacity of Earth; this planet could easily support ten or twenty billion people, perhaps even more. Technological and scientific progress has more than kept pace with population growth. As Francis Bacon predicted, thanks to technology and science, the lot of the masses has dramatically improved—especially in societies that have had the good sense to actively embrace industrialization.

In industrial societies, people are better nourished than ever before. Life expectancy is at its highest level ever, and it's still increasing. The physical environment we inhabit is generally becoming cleaner, not dirtier, as technological advances allow us to recycle materials and safely dispose of industry's non-recyclable residues.

Far from having to come to an end, economic growth can continue indefinitely. Economic growth is not based on an increasing consumption of scarce raw materials and energy, as the doomsayers would have us believe, but on technological and scientific advances. Optical fibers made of inexhaustible silicon that carry millions of phone calls have replaced wires made of scarce copper that carried only a few conversations. Computers made of cheap silicon chips and interconnected via optical fibers (the Internet) are replacing mail, journals, magazines, newspapers, and books. More information is being exchanged, yet fewer trees are needed for paper, less oil for airplanes, trains, and trucks.

Those alarmists who keep predicting that severe scarcity is just around the corner have been proven wrong time and again, not because resources are inexhaustible, but because we find cheaper and better ways of processing them or come up with substitutes that outperform their originals.

Some time ago, the late Julian Simon, author of *The Ultimate Resource* and an articulate spokesperson for continued economic and industrial growth, bet Paul Erlich, an environmental alarmist (*The Population Explosion*), that the price of copper would fall over the next five years. Simon easily won. The prices of most raw materials have steadily decreased for the last few hundred years. This widespread favorable trend is due to our hard-working machine partners, the bonanza of fossil-fuel energy they eat, and our accumulation of massive amounts of reliable information through science.

Understanding our reliance on fossil-fuel machines, some alarmists suggest that when oil supplies run low and oil prices skyrocket, the party will be over. Not so, counter the believers in our continued progress. Energy itself, they point out, has become cheaper over time. This trend will continue as safe nuclear fission and, especially, as clean, efficient, and inexhaustible solar and wind power replace and make oil power obsolete. High prices will conserve the remaining supplies of oil for use as feed stocks for the production of plastics and organic chemicals.

Great as the benefits from physical science and technology have been to date, these contributions will be dwarfed by the rapidly growing scientific benefits from the biotech revolution. No longer must we rely on crosses between the paltry numbers of species we can coax into interbreeding to improve our food supplies. Breaking down all genetic barriers, we'll be able to transfer desirable traits from one species to another, no matter how distantly related. We will have the power to create plants that thrive in farmlands previously lost to salination or desertification. Specially designed plants will provide their own fertilizer (nitrogen fixing) and pesticides. Farming, as it enters an era of factory-like mass production, will become so efficient that the amount of land devoted to agriculture will fall, even as our food supplies and population expand. Unlike the original agricultural revolution, when weeds, vermin, and microbes unfairly cashed in on civilization's artificial ecosystems, the biotech agricultural revolution will foil these opportunists, wreaking genetic havoc in their ranks.

The third era

Taking the long view of life on Earth, we might parse it into three eras. The first era would be life before the DNA encoding of information, an era when information and metabolism were one and the same thing. This first era probably lasted only a few hundred million years. The second is the DNA era of genetic evolution and selfish (not to mention cooperating) genes, which has lasted for almost four billion years. While the DNA era is still going strong, it now has a serious challenger. This third era is that of cultural evolution, an era of information that is separate from metabolism, separate from DNA, even increasingly separate from DNA-based organisms.

This isn't the first time that one form of life has forced other forms of life to adjust to its own selfish agenda. Such biological takeovers do occur on occasion, and they are often the major turning points in the evolution of life. As mentioned earlier, photosynthetic life revamped the planet over a billion years ago when it tapped an immense new source of power—the sun. It used solar energy to mine water for its hydrogen, releasing oxygen as a waste. This was a case of one life-form massively polluting the planet. Photosynthetic life established a new world order, forcing all other forms of life to adapt to the greatest pollution event of all time—the wholesale release of oxygen into the atmosphere. Oxygen physically transformed the planet, literally rusting the oceans by combining with iron to form iron oxide (rust), which sank to the ocean floors, creating the iron ores we now mine.

Similarly, cultural life has tapped into a new energy source—fossil fuels. Again, this source has poisonous byproducts, but we'll switch from fossil fuels to solar power or nuclear fusion long before we begin to approach the massive planet-changing pollution caused by early photosynthetic life. In humanity's case, there has indeed been a serious disruption of life on Earth as we've consumed massive amounts of fossil fuels, just as there was a massive disruption when photosynthetic life first took over. But, as before, life will evolve to cope with the transformed environment.

With the advantage of hindsight, we can state that the planetary grab by photosynthetic life was a good thing, that its massive oxygen pollution ended up being beneficial. Without oxygen and the high levels of energy release it enabled, few animals would have evolved. We can thank our lucky stars that some environmentally conservative do-gooder bacteria didn't talk the first photosynthetic experimenters out of their new high-tech process, citing its likeliness to despoil the environment. Who's to say that such great good won't happen again? Out of the current upheaval and destruction, out of the ongoing mass extinction of now-archaic life forms, new life could arise that transcends it all. Perhaps our machines, by utilizing the vast, previously untouched stores of fossil fuels, are the new photosynthetic life, running out of control, changing the planet forever in beneficial ways.

Planetary superorganism

In any event, Earth's era of cultural evolution is now well underway. We humans, together with our indispensable machine partners and domesticated plants and animals, are the winners in the new pecking order. Other life forms are the losers—they need to adjust to us, not we to them. We're in charge of evolution now. Except perhaps among the weeds and their microbial ilk, traditional Darwinian evolution is no longer of much significance on this planet. Agriculture has already overwhelmed the vast majority of the natural world. Natural selection, for the most part, has been replaced by human selection. As the take-charge winners, we've become even more successful than the highly organized, hard working ants.

Ants were rarely able to build beyond city-states—colonies of about five million ants with the combined weight of a cow. True, a few ant species formed empires of sorts, but such empires failed to take hold and remained only rare curiosities. Not so with human city-states. Shortly after they were formed, they coalesced into empires, super-superorganisms that competed at a far higher level, pitting entire sections of the planet against one another. Today, we're witnessing the emergence of the first planetary superorganism, a life-form that is harnessing the entire planet for its own benefit. Sadly, winners imply losers; the planetary pie is only so large.

It's easy to feel sorry for the losers. We naturally cheer for the underdogs. Yet hard choices must be made. As the biomass of we humans and our domesticated plants and animals has increased, the biomass of other species has inevitably decreased. As we have made their habitats our own, the variety of life has necessarily narrowed. Natural ecosystems have now been replaced, wholesale, with human-dominated ecosystems. We are the new nature. Life not adapted to the planet's new, dominant type of ecosystem is on the wane. How could it be otherwise? It's not at all clear that this is bad; wouldn't the planet be as well off with a million species as with 50 million? Do we really need 500,000 species of beetles? We should take the advice of Genesis 1:26: "Be fertile and increase, fill the Earth and master it."

In spite of our near-total victory, we have magnanimously set wildlife preserves aside to preserve the outmoded losers—life that's unable to compete in an ecosystem designed for human benefit. This is certainly a noble first in life's long history on this planet. Cultural evolution is kinder than relentless genetics which is commonly thought of as "red in tooth and claw."

Just as there are winner and loser animal and plant species with respect to the new human-dominated planet, there are also winner and loser human societies. Some societies are having increasing difficulty coming to grips with the modern world; in fact, they seem to be purposely shunning capitalistic industrialization, globalization, and democracy. Clinging to corrupt or authoritative regimes, extolling religious fundamentalism, actively opposing rationalism, capitalism, science, and freedom of the press, these countries appear to be purposely handicapping themselves just as competition has heated up planet-wide. Because accelerating change is the hallmark of the modern era, countries that can handle such change will prosper at the expense of those unable to do so. Evolution continues ever onward with cultural evolution now in the driver's seat. Get with it or be left behind and be relegated to an exhibit in the zoo.

As the biotech revolution swings into high gear, food production will increasingly resemble industrial processes. Already, we've replaced sugar cane with an entirely artificial chemical, isoglucose. As demand for old-style, agriculturally grown food falls off, the economic position of low-tech countries will only worsen. Unless they get with the program and rapidly emulate the West's high-tech ways, industrial powers may have to write them off, allowing them to collapse and be re-colonized at some later date. Civilized humanity, after all, has already replaced recalcitrant hunter-gatherer societies that refused to hop on the bandwagon.

All together on the global farm

For those with eyes to see, the future has already begun. The planetary superorganism has already arrived; a global, cosmopolitan culture has coalesced among the industrialized societies. Although this global culture's roots lie in the West, other regions have also contributed their vital shares, and Asian countries such as China, Japan, and India are becoming increasingly influential.

National leaders no longer have the clout or significance they once had. Power has moved to multi-national corporations and to a multitude of decentralized but highly efficient decision-makers interconnected by rapid global communications. The world economy is in charge; economic efficiency now reigns supreme. The ants, if only they could speak, would approve!

Those countries and regions that are doing well in the new world system have the accumulated knowledge of humanity at their fingertips, a well-educated work force to access it, and the capital, financial structures, and entrepreneurs to pull it all together. The vast stores of information accrued by civilizations and by science suggest a starkly different outcome from boom and bust: instead of attempting to restrain ourselves and fit in with other life forms, we will continue to restructure them and the planet's ecosystems to suit our own pioneering civilizations, our rapidly emerging planetary superorganism.

Cultural humanity was the breakthrough life needed to reach a higher level of complexity, to move beyond DNA-bound insect superorganisms to effective empires and a true planetary superorganism. This breakthrough, like many others, involved a merger—in this case the three-way global partnership of humans, domesticated plants and animals, and machines. We are all pulling together now, working together in harmony down on the global farm.

Chapter 12

STAR TREK
Our descendants inherit the galaxy

We have a moral obligation to survive—a responsibility to see to it that this grand experiment called intelligent life does not end.

Eric Chaisson

The only people who really felt the tug,
the gravitational attraction, of outer space,
were the dreamers, the trekkies,
and various Californians.

Joel Achenback

Eyes on the stars

The three alternative futures we've considered so far—Chimpanzee Paradise, Boom and Bust, and Planetary Superorganism—have one feature in common: all are Earth-centered. As far as these futures are concerned, Copernicus, Galileo, and Kepler—who freed us from our geocentric mindset—need never have been born. Humanity's brilliant discoveries of the past century or so—that stars are distant suns, that our sun is but one among billions in our galaxy, that there is an essentially infinite set of galaxies—all are irrelevant, immaterial, and mere curiosities.

From the viewpoint of these three futures, our brave venture into space amounts to little more than overgrown boys playing with their expensive toys. So what if Yuri Gagarin circled the Earth and Neil Armstrong stepped onto the Moon? Who really cares that we sent clever machines for close-up views of other planets, that rovers roamed the barren surface of Mars, and that giant telescopes have recently discovered scores of planets orbiting distant suns?

And what of our dreams of traveling to distant stars, of surviving beyond the short lifetime of our local star and planet, of meeting other intelligent life in the cosmos? There's no room in the parochial futures we have considered so far for these dreams; they assume our fate is, one way or another, forever bound to that of Earth and its life. Our species was born of and will die on planet Earth. Our human adventure is strictly local in space and limited in time. We'll be gone long before our sun turns into a red giant and consumes our birth planet. Our cosmic dreams are mere Hollywood fantasies.

Star Trek, our fourth and final illustrative future, firmly rejects such spirit-crushing limitations. Our final future is grand in scope, cosmic in its vision. It celebrates our scientific accomplishments, applauds and honors our machine partners. It continues our species' adventure—an adventure that began when we made our first stone tools, when we spilled out of Africa, an adventure that will continue as we head out from planet Earth into our galaxy, as we search for life and intelligence elsewhere in the universe. Star Trek is a positive future with a vision: humanity will form the ultimate level of organized complexity—a galactic superorganism.

Homes away from home

This idea of humanity spreading throughout our galaxy makes the presumption that there actually are planets around other stars, and that some of them are, in fact, sufficiently earth-like for us to inhabit. The detection of "extra-solar" planets is quite recent, but already we feel less alone in their presence. How did we find these far away planets?

Rather than looking for planets directly—their faint reflected light is totally overwhelmed by the bright light of their nearby parent stars—astronomers concentrated their efforts on measuring slight changes in the wavelengths of the light the stars themselves emitted. If a planet circles a star and the star wobbles back and forth as a result, then the star's light will ever so slightly shift its wavelength back and forth due to the Doppler Effect. This shift is toward the blue when the planet pulls the star towards us and toward the red when the planet pulls the star away from us. Even with Jupiter-sized planets in orbits close to a star—which maximizes the Doppler shift—astronomers at first expected the effect to be barely detectable. On the contrary, the Doppler shift technique has been the bulwark of our search for extrasolar planets. There are other ways to detect distant planets however, and one of these—planetary transits—has discovered several planets.

Almost two hundred extrasolar planets have been now discovered. We have yet to detect any planets as small as the Earth nor do we expect to for a few years—they're simply beyond our current detection capabilities. Still, as our techniques improve and data accumulate, we're finding ever-smaller planets at greater orbital distances from their parent stars. We hope that a significant percentage of planetary systems will be similar to our own, with the gas giants in their outer orbits and terrestrial-type planets, including Earth look-alikes, in inner orbits.

Getting there

Even if we assume that many other earth-like planets exist in our galaxy, how might we travel to them? There are at least two versions of interstellar travel: one with warp drive and one without. In view of our current scientific knowledge, warp drive is clearly only possible on the imaginative set of *Star Trek*. Still, as warp-drive advocates are quick to point out, there may be physical laws we know nothing about that could make warp drive or other fantastic means of travel possible, even practical.

If, however, we assume that warp drive is strictly for Hollywood, then, while not impossible, interstellar travel would be rather time consuming, to say the least. If ships traveled between stars at a leisurely pace—less than one-tenth the speed of light—or if they traveled greater distances than just to our neighboring stars, then travel time could easily exceed the lifetimes of the human travelers. This suggests the use of generational arks—colonies traveling through space in gigantic, self-contained starships—or suspended animation of some sort, as in the classic science fiction movie, *Alien*.

At one-tenth the speed of light, it would still take nearly a lifetime to travel one way to the nearest star, and much longer to slow-boat to the nearest earth-like planet (the nearest star is unlikely to harbor planets that would support life). If we could travel at nearly the speed of light, we could cut the journey down to a measly few years—even fewer from the viewpoint of the traveler, thanks to the time-dilation effect of Special Relativity. No matter how long it takes to travel to distant terrestrial-type planets however, the burning question arises. Will we find life out there?

Life on Mars

Now that we're discovering extrasolar planets by the score, many scientists are optimistic that we'll eventually find signs of extraterrestrial life. There are even a few scientists who believe we have already found some fossil evidence of Martian life contained in a meteorite. This meteorite was blasted from Mars into space millions of years ago and eventually wound up in Antarctica.

Mars, for many years, seemed a likely abode for life. In the late 1800s, Percival Lowell founded the Lowell Observatory to study Mars from the clear skies of Flagstaff, Arizona. He believed he saw faint signs of canals on Mars, and he hypothesized that Mars was home to an advanced civilization conserving its dwindling water resources via a planet-wide system of canals. Mars, Lowell believed, was a dying planet. He was correct about that, although it probably died a few billion years earlier than he had in mind. He was wrong about the canals, however. They were just one of those honest illusions that happen when one strains the limits of human perception.

Interest in Mars picked up as we entered the space age. Although early probes sent to Mars revealed a cratered landscape somewhat reminiscent of our Moon's, there seemed to be a good possibility that simple life might have adapted to the worsening environment over the years, and might still exist in hardy forms just below the surface. This may indeed be the case, although the two Viking probes that landed on Mars in 1976 failed to find any evidence of life.

In recent years, we've been able to take a close look at Mars via robotic explorers. Analysis strongly suggests that Mars, in an earlier time, had sizeable oceans and flowing rivers—conditions appropriate for life. Although extant Martian subterranean life is still a possibility, it's even more likely that simple life once existed on Mars but has been extinct now for several billions of years.

Life is tough

On a cosmic time scale, life on earth appeared very shortly after physical conditions made it possible. Although some controversy still surrounds the earliest fossils and traces of organic matter, it's likely that life appeared within just a few hundred million years of the point in Earth's geological evolution when our planet had settled down enough to form permanent oceans. The probable conclusion is that there's a good chance that life will appear with relative dispatch on other planets once conditions for its formation are favorable.

Not only did life form quickly on Earth, it apparently did so in what we would now consider a decidedly hostile environment—one of withering heat. The tree of life appears, at its very roots, to have consisted of hyperthermophiles—bacterial lovers of heat. We first discovered these strange bacteria still living comfortably in boiling-hot springs and geysers.

Another recent and surprising discovery was entire colonies of life living in total darkness at very high temperatures and pressures around mid-ocean volcanic vents. Some scientists believe that life might actually have begun at these vents. At the other extreme of low temperatures and high altitudes, life has also been found under rocks in the very dry valleys of Antarctica. Life has even been found within permanently iced-over lakes. Clearly, life can exist in a much broader range of environments than we previously thought possible.

The demonstrated ability of life to survive and perhaps even originate in extreme environments has reshaped the thinking of astrobiologists—those scientists who study life beyond Earth—about what constitutes a "habitable zone" around a star. These zones have been greatly widened to match our new understanding of the hardiness of life. Furthermore, the life we've observed at mid-ocean ridges has encouraged speculation that extraterrestrial life may not even need a planetary surface *per se* for its origin and sustenance; it could develop in complete darkness in such exotic locations as Europa, one of Jupiter's moons.

Europa has no atmosphere and is covered with ice—not a likely prospect for life under the old paradigm—but a sea under the ice with possible volcanic vents gives Europa definite possibilities in the new life-is-tough paradigm.

An interesting sidelight is the suggestion that terrestrial-sized planets could, during the final formation of a planetary system, be scattered into outer space like so many billiard balls. This could happen when a hot Jupiter spirals in towards the central star from the system's outer regions, acting like a cue ball. Some of these scattered terrestrial planets could contain enough radioactive material to keep their cores molten and oceans liquid for billions of years as they drifted alone through the darkness of interstellar space. It is possible that life on such a warm but dark planet might develop at mid-ocean vents, evolve, and spread across the land, perhaps even becoming intelligent. If the planet's atmosphere were clear, then presumably these creatures would have superbly night-adapted eyes. They would, presumably, make wonderful astronomers!

Cosmic ecology

Our current understanding of life suggests that it is most likely to form under conditions where there is liquid water, a supply of carbon, and a fairly gentle and steady flow of energy. Our best bets, modern thinking suggests, are terrestrial-type planets of sufficient mass to retain a substantial atmosphere that are also situated an appropriate distance from their parent stars to maintain significant oceans of water. If a planet is too close to its star, it would be too hot on the surface of the planet for liquid oceans to form, while if it is too far away, any oceans would soon freeze solid in the cold. The orbital distances between too hot and too cold define the maximum habitable zone around a star, though there are many additional factors that bear on habitability, as we shall see.

When it comes to habitability, not all galaxies are created equal, nor are all locations within a given galaxy equally favorable. Larger stars, the ones that run through their life cycles quickly and explode as supernovae, are rare in elliptical galaxies and in the central regions of spiral galaxies. As a result, the interstellar media in these galaxies or regions is not significantly enriched with elements heavier than hydrogen and helium. The heavier elements, such as iron, silicon, and oxygen, are crucial to the formation of terrestrial-type planets and life itself. Furthermore, the central regions of many spiral galaxies are as hyperactive and crowded as Los Angeles freeways at rush hour, with stars moving at high velocity in tight orbits. However, this still leaves all the non-central regions of spiral galaxies where, as luck would have it, the bulk of the stars reside.

Stars can also contribute to or undermine their planet's habitability. Massive stars are very hot and bright, radiating prodigious amounts of energy at ultraviolet wavelengths. This energy flow is so intense that it would be disruptive to the fragile chemistry of any incipient life. In any event, massive stars have short lives that end in spectacular supernovae explosions—hardly conducive to the extended evolution of life! Life, without doubt, favors kinder, gentler stars. However, the contributions toward the enrichment of the interstellar media that massive stars have made during their death throes are vital to life. Thank you supernovae, for your life-giving gift.

At the other end of the stellar spectrum are small, faint, miserly stars that meter out their energy so slowly they can live for trillions or even tens of trillions of years. These stars radiate primarily in the red end of the visible wavelengths and also in the near infrared. While massive stars are rare, these diminutive stars are quite common, easily forming the majority of stars in our galaxy as well as the universe at large. Their gentle, long-lived ways would seem ideal for life. But there appears to be a Catch-22 involved with any possibly habitable planets around these stars.

Because the light from these stars is so faint, planets only a modest distance from them would freeze solid. In other words, the habitable zones of these diminutive stars do not extend out very far. Unfortunately for life, as a planet's orbit moves ever closer to a central star, a tidal-lock-in effect eventually kicks in and causes the planet to rotate about its star with one side always facing inwards, a situation similar to that of Earth's own moon. The side of the planet always facing the star roasts while the other side freezes, unless there's an atmosphere thick enough to efficiently distribute the heat around the entire planet.

What are the possibilities for life on a tidally locked-in planet with a thick, heat-circulating atmosphere? Land on the side of the planet facing the star might be covered with thick forests. The leaves on these trees would be permanently pointed in the direction of the "sun," a direction that would never change. It would be the ultimate Land of the Midnight Sun. On the planet's permanent night side there would, presumably, be no photosynthetic life, but there might be life of other sorts, living off the nutrients from the sunlit side brought over by ocean currents. Perhaps someone's already written a science fiction story that describes this strange world.

Stars suitable for habitable planets appear to be a Goldilocks-type story—not too large and not too small. Stars like our sun last long enough for life to develop and, at the same time, have habitable zones that generally lie well beyond the point of tidal lock-in. While such stars do not form a majority in our galaxy, they do constitute a significant minority. They are consequently plentiful enough to make numerous habitable planets a real possibility.

Searching for Intelligent Life

Humans haven't only initiated the search for planets and simple life elsewhere in the cosmos, but we are also keeping an eye out for intelligent life. Early efforts to find signs of intelligent life beyond Earth used the reception of radio signals at the turn of the past century. In 1901, Nikola Tesla (1856-1943), the Croatian-born electrical engineer who did more than anyone else to bring us alternating current, claimed he had detected signals from extra-terrestrial (ET) intelligent life with one of his giant wire coils, now known as Tesla coils. Nor was Tesla alone in such claims. Guglielmo Marconi (1874-1943), the father of radio, also said he'd detected such signals. These claims were never substantiated, and it's now thought that both Tesla and Marconi were listening to "whistlers," the long-distance radio waves generated by massive thunderstorms continents away.

These and similar false starts aside, the real, concerted scientific search for intelligent life in the universe began with the 1959 publication by two Cornell University physicists, Giuseppe Cocconi and Philip Morrison, of a paper in the prestigious science journal *Nature*. In their paper, they pointed out that interstellar communication was (barely) possible with technology no more advanced than our own. Recognizing that our technical civilization was in its infancy, they proposed that there might be more advanced civilizations beyond Earth with the power to purposely operate radio beacons that would announce their presence. They even suggested a wavelength on which radio telescopes should listen, that of neutral hydrogen. Neutral hydrogen has a wavelength that radio astronomers in any civilization would be likely to utilize to explore the vast clouds of hydrogen in our galaxy.

Cocconi and Morrison failed, at first, to entice any radio astronomers to search for signals from extraterrestrial civilizations. Then, Frank Drake, a young radio astronomer just starting his career, initiated the first search at the National Radio Observatory in Green Bank, West Virginia. Using Green Bank's new eighty-five foot diameter radio telescope, he searched for signals from the vicinity of two nearby, sun-like stars. Although Drake didn't receive any signals, his search was scientific in spirit, technically sound, and impressed many other scientists.

Drake's initial search was followed, in 1961—also at Green Bank—by the first scientific meeting on the topic of intelligent life beyond Earth. Besides Cocconi, Morrison, and Drake, Carl Sagan and five others, including the dolphin intelligence researcher John Lilly, attended the meeting. The purpose of the meeting was to "examine the prospects for the existence of other societies in the galaxy with whom communications might be possible; to attempt an estimate of their number; to consider some of the technical problems involved in the establishment of communication; and to examine ways in which our understanding of the problem might be improved." Drake's pioneering observations and the meeting at Green Bank launched SETI, the Search for Extra-Terrestrial Intelligence.

Since the first modest attempts at Green Bank, SETI has significantly expanded, first under the generous auspices of NASA, then with private funding when Congress, thanks to Senator Proxmire's Golden Fleece Award, blocked any further government support of SETI. Currently, the bulk of the searching is done in a "piggyback" mode on the giant radio telescopes at Arecibo in Puerto Rico and the Parkes radio telescope in Australia. In this mode, SETI scientists make do with looking for signals from the direction of stars radio astronomers happen to be researching. However, a new radio telescope dedicated to the search—the Allen Array—is under construction.

Our descendants inherit the galaxy

Our search for planets, life, and intelligence elsewhere will continue. Our first tentative steps away from our birth planet will grow over time as we explore our own solar system and then travel to distant stars. We are an adventurous species, and it is our fate to inherit the galaxy. The universe is young, still in its infancy. Yet, in only fourteen billion years, the cosmos has evolved from simple energy to intelligent life that understands how it came to be. Thoughts of what the cosmos might accomplish in its next fourteen billion years overwhelm our minds.

Humanity will spearhead evolution to ever higher levels of complexity. We clever chimpanzees of planet Earth, along with our machine partners, will spread out across the Milky Way Galaxy—numerous as the ants that inspired us—to become the ultimate organized complexity, a galactic superorganism.

EPILOGUE
Futures most likely and desirable

A perpetual stream toward richness, diversity, and complexity,
the outcome of which cannot be foreseen,
may be the true fate of the universe.
Eric Chaisson

For my part I know nothing with any certainty,
but the sight of the stars makes me dream.
Vincent van Gogh

I occasionally present my grand scientific story of humanity as a one-hour talk at high schools and universities. Afterward, I ask the students which of the four futures they consider to be most likely. They invariably elect *Boom and Bust* by an overwhelming, nearly unanimous majority. Considering any other future as strikes them as unrealistic and wishful thinking. With respect to recent environmental initiatives, students see them as too little, too late. Some cynically suggest that these environmental initiatives are mainly multinational public relations campaigns that the world's governments and multinational corporations put on while they finish raping the planet.

The first time I asked audiences which future was most desirable, as opposed to most likely, I expected a solid vote for Chimpanzee Paradise. After all, if they thought a crash was most likely one would think they would want a future that was furthest from a crash, a distinctly planet-friendly future. This didn't happen—at least not unanimously. The vote was split, almost evenly, between Chimpanzee Paradise and Star Trek. Why, I asked? Some students wanted us rejoin nature as ordinary citizens, while others wanted us to continue our exciting, Star-Trekish adventure as Masters of the Universe. Several students who voted for Star Trek suggested that Chimpanzee Paradise would be boring and somewhat mindless. How, in any event, they asked, would we ever get our population down to millions without a bust or unpalatable application of raw force?

Then the students—turnabout being fair play—insisted on hearing my views. Here, for what it is worth, are my thoughts on the matter. I contend that a crash is unlikely, at least one that eliminates *Homo sapiens* altogether. We're a tenacious species, and the planet's ecosystems are tough. With twenty billion humans, however, some lucky microbe could break the code to cashing in on the ultimate biological jackpot. This would create a spectacular crash, but I expect we would survive the crash, our knowledge and technology intact enough to figure out how to ward off similar future disasters.

Although Chimpanzee Paradise is probably just a utopian fantasy, Star Trek would continue life's unbroken record of information accumulation, advancing itself to a new, high in the hierarchy of complexity. Considering the past track record of life, and the current wild burst of energy shown by cultural evolution, it appears to me that an evolutionary breakthrough has been made that ranks right up there with the first DNA life or the first photosynthetic life. We are living in the midst of a massive evolutionary radiation, a virtual explosion of human and machine specialization.

As a species, I believe we face two challenges. Our first challenge is to avoid becoming victims of our own success; our second is to safely venture forth from our birth planet to habitable homes circling distant stars. I call these two challenges, respectively, the Greenie Challenge and the Trekkie Challenge. These challenges are interrelated and interdependent, for it will take us a long time to reach the stars. Meanwhile, we must take good care of our only home, planet Earth.

Green preservation, green self-control is vital, but it isn't enough for us. We also need our Trekkie vision of a grand and glorious future. We are a venturesome species, and we dream of immortality, of the cosmos. Thus, our green thumbs and starry eyes naturally go together. Greenies and Trekkies, hand in hand, arm in arm, will lead us to our destiny.

In the future I envision, we will do the un-evolutionary thing. We will restrain ourselves and won't chop down the last forests, won't pump the last water from our aquifers or the last oil from their black underground lakes. But how long will it take to change the course of evolution? The inertia of cultural evolution is so strong, the power of multinationals and of short-term profits so overwhelming; the needs of our millions to eat, to make a living, and to produce offspring are so pressing.

We are, in fact, already changing evolution. We're rapidly becoming consciously thoughtful planetary citizens, even cosmic citizens. It was only a few decades ago when we first realized we were facing planetary limits. Now there are thousands, perhaps even hundreds of thousands, of planet-saving initiatives. Saving the Earth through self-restraint is a major growth industry. Green institutes have sprung up like wildflowers after a spring rain. Humanity is rapidly responding to recognition of the planetary limits to our growth. Multinational corporations now talk about and are increasingly working on their triple bottom line: economic efficiency, enriched human resources, and environmental sustainability. We humans are greatly concerned about nuclear proliferation, and we're taking action to prevent it. Democracy is spreading; there are even the beginnings of a global democracy. Universal education is spreading; women are becoming empowered.

We are rising to the stern evolutionary challenge of self-restraint, and we're going to make it through the turbulent straits of this major evolutionary shift. By the year 3000, we'll be well on the other side of the transition from genetic- to cultural-evolutionary dominance. We will have made it through the "bottleneck" of challenges to planetary superorganism.

What will concern us in the year 3000? Not sustainability; we'll have solved that problem long ago. Not population; it will have been stable at a comfortable level for centuries. Not nuclear weapons; they'll have become a rapidly fading bad memory.

So what *will* concern us? We will be concerned with discovery, with investigating the life we have detected on planets around other stars, and with solving the daunting problems presented by interstellar travel. I believe that we are destined to leave the planet of our birth, to spread to other stellar systems in this little corner of our galaxy—perhaps eventually to the entire galaxy. We are destined to live beyond the short life of our local star, the Sun. The universe is young, we are young, and our cosmic future stretches before us—an immense banquet we will savor for eons.

FURTHER READING

PREFACE Story, science, and synthesis

Altschuler, Daniel. 2002. *Children of the Stars: Our Origin, Evolution and Destiny.* Cambridge: Cambridge University Press.

Bryson, Bill. 2003. *A Short History of Nearly Everything.* New York: Broadway Books.

Chaisson, Eric. 2001. *Cosmic Evolution: The Rise of Complexity in Nature.* Cambridge: Harvard University Press.

_______. 2006. *Epic of Evolution: Seven Ages of the Cosmos.* New York: Columbia University Press.

Christian, David. 2004 *Maps of Time: An Introduction to Big History.* Berkeley: University of California Press.

Delsemme, Armand. 1998. *Our Cosmic Origins: From the Big Bang to the Emergence of Life and Intelligence.* Cambridge: Cambridge University Press.

Reeves, Hubert. 1991. *The Hour of Our Delight: Cosmic Evolution, Order, and Complexity.* New York: W. H. Freeman.

Sagan, Carl. 1980. *Cosmos.* New York: Wing Books.

Seielstad, George. 1983. *Cosmic Ecology: The View from the Outside In.* Berkeley: University of California Press.

Shapley, Harlow. 1958. *Of Stars and Men: The Human Response to an Expanding Universe.* London: Elek Books.

Swimme, Brian, and Thomas Berry. 1992. *The Universe Story: From the Primordial Flaring Forth to the Ecozoic Era—A Celebration of the Unfolding of the Cosmos.* San Francisco: HarperCollins.

Chapter 1

COSMOS Stars and Planets for Life

Chown, Marcus. 1999. *The Magic Furnace: The Search for the Origins of Atoms*. London: Jonathan Cape.

Ferguson, Kitty 1998. *Measuring the Universe: Our Historic Quest to Chart the Horizons of Space and Time.* New York: Walker.

Gingerich, Owen. 1993. *The Eye of Heaven: Ptolemy, Copernicus, Kepler.* New York: American Institute of Physics.

Goldsmith, Donald. 1995. *Einstein's Greatest Blunder? The Cosmological Constant and Other Fudge Factors in the Physics of the Universe.* Cambridge: Harvard University Press.

_______. 2000. *The Runaway Universe: The Race to Find the Future of the Cosmos.* Cambridge: Perseus.

Hearnshaw, John B. 1986. *The Analysis of Starlight: One Hundred and Fifty Years of Astronomical Spectroscopy.* Cambridge: Cambridge University.

Hubble, Edwin P. 1925. Cepheids in Spiral Nebulae. *Publications of the American Astronomical Society,* 5:261-264; reprinted in *Observatory,* 48: 139-142.

Kaler, James B. 1992. *Stars.* New York: Scientific American.

Rees, Martin. 1997. *Before the Beginning: Our Universe and Others.* New York: W. H. Freeman.

Weinberg, Steven. 1997. *The First Three Minutes: A Modern View of the Origin of the Universe.* New York: Basic Books.

Chapter 2

LIFE Nature's road to complexity

Allman, John. 1999. *Evolving Brains.* New York: Scientific American Library.

Baba, Jeffrey, and Christopher Wills. 2000. *The Spark of Life: Darwin and the Primeval Soup.* Cambridge: Perseus.

Barlow, Connie, ed. 1994. *Evolution Extended: Biological Debates on the Meaning of Life.* Cambridge: MIT Press.

Benton, Michael. 2003. *When Life Nearly Died: The Greatest Mass Extinction of All Time.* London: Thames and Hudson.

Bonner, John T. 1988. *The Evolution of Complexity by Means of Natural Selection.* Princeton: Princeton University Press.

Corning, Peter. 2003. *Nature's Magic: Synergy in Evolution and the Fate of Humankind.* New York: Oxford University Press.

Cziko, Gary. 1995. *Without Miracles: Universal Selection Theory and the Second Darwinian Revolution*. Cambridge: MIT Press.

Dawkins, Richard. 1989. *The Selfish Gene*, 2d ed. Oxford: Oxford University.

_______. 1995. *River Out of Eden: A Darwinian View of Life*. New York: Basic Books.

_______. 1996. *Climbing Mount Improbable*. New York: W.W. Norton.

Depew, David J., and Bruce H. Weber. 1995. *Darwinism Evolving: System Dynamics and the Genealogy of Natural Selection*. Cambridge: MIT Press.

Dugathkin, Lee. 1997. *Cooperation Among Animals: An Evolutionary Perspective*. New York: Oxford University Press.

_______. 1999. *Cheating Monkeys and Citizen Bees: The Nature of Cooperation in Animals and Humans*. New York: Free Press.

_______. 2000. *The Imitation Factor: Evolution Beyond the Gene*. New York: The Free Press.

Duve, Christian de. 1995. *Vital Dust: Life as a Cosmic Imperative*. New York: HarperCollins.

Dyson, Freeman. 1999. *Origins of Life*, 2nd ed . New York: Harper Colophon.

Fortey, Richard. 1998. *Life: A Natural History of the First Four Billion Years of Life on Earth*. New York: HarperCollins.

Fry, Iris. 2000. *The Emergence of Life on Earth: A Historical and Scientific Overview*. New Brunswick: Rutgers University Press.

Gould, Stephen, J. 1989. *Wonderful Life: The Burgess Shale and the Nature of History*. London: Burnett.

Gross, Michael. 1996. *Life on the Edge: Amazing Creatures Thriving in Extreme Environments*. Cambridge: Perseus.

Lewin, Roger. 1999. *Patterns in Evolution: The New Molecular View*. New York: Scientific American Library.

Maynard Smith, John, and Eors Szathmáry. 1995. *The Major Transitions in Evolution*. Cambridge: Cambridge University Press.

_______. 1999. *The Origins of Life: From the Birth of Life to the Origin of Language*. New York: Oxford University Press.

Margulis, Lynn. 1984. *Early Life*. Boston: Jones and Bartlett.

Margulis, Lynn, and Dorian Sagan. 1995. *What Is Life?* New York: Simon & Schuster.

Michod, Richard E. 1999. *Darwinian Dynamics: Evolutionary Transitions in Fitness and Individuality.* Princeton: Princeton University Press.

Morowitz, Harold. 1983. *Beginnings of Cellular Life: Metabolism Recapitulates Biogenesis.* New Haven: Yale University Press.

Morris, Simon Conway. 1998. *The Crucible of Creation.* New York: Oxford University Press.

_______. 2003. *Life's Solution: Inevitable Humans in a Lonely Universe.* New York: Cambridge University Press.

Parker, Andrew. 2003. *In the Blink of an Eye.* Cambridge: Perseus.

Petterson, Max. 1996. *Complexity and Evolution.* Cambridge: Cambridge University Press.

Plotkin, Henry. 1993. *Darwin Machines and the Nature of Knowledge.* Cambridge: Harvard University Press.

Postgate, John. 1994. *The Outer Reaches of Life.* New York: Cambridge University Press.

Chapter 3

ANTS Jewels of the genetic crown

Agosta, William. 1992. *Chemical Communication: The Language of Pheromones.* New York: Scientific American Library.

Colinvaux, Paul. 1978. *Why Big Fierce Animals Are Rare.* Princeton: Princeton University Press.

Gordon, Deborah. 1999. *Ants at Work: How An Insect Society Is Organized.* New York: Free Press.

Gould, James L., and Carol Grant Gould. 1995. *The Honey Bee.* New York: Scientific American Library.

Haskins, Caryl. 1939. *Of Ants and Men.* New York: Prentice-Hall.

Holldobler, Bert, and Edward O. Wilson. 1990. *The Ants.* Cambridge: Harvard University Press.

_______. 1994. *Journey to the Ants: A Story of Scientific Exploration.* Cambridge: Harvard University Press.

Hoyt, Erich. 1996. *The Earth Dwellers: Adventures in the Land of Ants.* New York: Simon and Schuster.

Marais, Eugène. 1973. *The Soul of the White Ant*. Baltimore: Penguin Books.

Wilson, Edward. 1971. *The Insect Societies.* Cambridge: Harvard University Press.

_______. 1975. *Sociology.* Abridged ed. Cambridge: Harvard University. Press.

Chapter 4

CHIMPANZEES Masters of Machiavellian intrigue

Boesch, Christophe, and Hedwige Boesch-Achermann. 2000. The *Chimpanzees of the Tai Forest: Behavioral Ecology and Evolution.* New York: Oxford University Press.

Bonner, John Tyler. 1980. *The Evolution of Culture in Animals.* Princeton: Princeton University Press.

Cheney, Dorothy L., and Robert M. Seyfarth. 1990. *How Monkeys See the World.* Chicago: University of Chicago Press.

Diamond, Jared. 1992. *The Third Chimpanzee: The Evolution and Future of the Human Animal.* New York: HarperCollins.

Fossey, Dian. 1983. *Gorillas in the Mist.* Boston: Houghton Mifflin.

Galdikas, Birute. 1995. *Reflections of Eden: My Years with the Orangutans of Borneo.* Boston: Little, Brown.

Goodall, Jane. 1977. *In the Shadow of Man.* Boston: Houghton Mifflin Company.

_______. 1990. *Through a Window: My Thirty Years with the Chimpanzees of Gombe.* Boston: Houghton Mifflin.

Gould, James, and Carol Gould. 1994. *The Animal Mind.* New York: Scientific American Library.

Griffin, Donald. 1992. *Animal Minds.* Chicago: University of Chicago Press.

McGrew, William C. 1992. *Chimpanzee Material Culture: Implications for Human Evolution.* New York: Cambridge University Press.

McGrew, William C., Linda F. Marchant, and Toshisada Nishida, eds. 1996. *Great Ape Societies.* New York: Cambridge University Press.

Parker, Sue T., and Kathleen R. Gibson. 1990. *"Language" and Intelligence in Monkeys and Apes.* Baltimore: Johns Hopkins University Press.

Parker, Sue T., R. W. Mitchell, and M. L. Boccia. 1994. *Self-Awareness in Animals and Humans*. Baltimore: Johns Hopkins University Press.

Stanford, Craig B. 1999. *The Hunting Apes: Meat Eating and the Origins of Human Behavior*. Princeton: Princeton University Press.

Strum, Shirley C. 1987. *Almost Human: A Journey into the World of Baboons*. London: Elm Tree.

Trefil, James. 1997. *Are We Unique?* New York: John Wiley & Sons, Inc.

Van Schaik, Carel. 2004. *Among Orangutans: Red Apes and the Rise of Human Culture*. Cambridge: Harvard University Press.

Waal, Frans de. 1982. *Chimpanzee Politics: Power and Sex among Apes.* Baltimore: John Hopkins University.

______. 1989. *Peacemaking among Primates*. Cambridge: Harvard University Press.

______. 1996. *Good Natured: The Origins of Right and Wrong In Humans and Other Animals*. Cambridge: Harvard University Press.

Waal, Frans de, and Frans Lanting. 1997. *Bonobo: The Forgotten Ape*. Berkeley: University of California Press.

Wrangham, Richard W., W. C. McGrew, Frans de Waal, and Paul G. Heltne, eds. 1994. *Chimpanzee Cultures*. Cambridge: Harvard University Press.

Wrangham, Richard, and Dale Peterson. 1996. *Demonic Males: Apes and the Origins of Human Violence.* Boston: Houghton Mifflin Company.

Chapter 5

HOMINIDS The chimpanzees who were thrown to the lions

Alcock, John. 2001. *The Triumph of Sociobiology.* New York: Oxford University Press.

Allman, William F. 1994. *The Stone Age Present: How Evolution Has Shaped Modern Life*. New York: Simon & Schuster.

Bikerton, D. 1995. *Language and Human Behavior*. Seattle: University of Washington.

Blackmore, Susan. 1999. *The Meme Machine.* New York: Oxford University Press.

Boehm, Christopher. 1999. *Hierarchy in the Forest: The Evolution of Egalitarian Behavior.* Cambridge: Harvard University Press.

Boyd, Robert, and Peter J. Richerson. 1985. *Culture and the Evolutionary Process.* Chicago: The University of Chicago Press.

_______. 2002. *Not by Genes Alone: The Nature of Cultures.* Chicago: University of Chicago Press.

Cavalli-Sforza, L. L. 1995. *The Great Human Diasporas: The History of Diversity and Evolution.* Reading: Addison-Wesley.

Corballis, Michael C. 1991. *The Lopsided Ape: Evolution of the Generative Mind.* Oxford: Oxford University.

Corballis, Michael C., and Stephen E. G. Lea. 1999. *The Descent of Mind: Psychological Perspectives on Hominid Evolution.* New York: Oxford University Press.

Deacon, Terrence W. 1997. *The Symbolic Species: The Co-Evolution of Language and the Brain.* New York: W. W. Norton.

Donald, Merlin. 2001. *A Mind So Rare: The Evolution of Human Consciousness.* New York: Oxford Universtiy Press

Dunbar, Robin. 1996. *Grooming, Gossip, and the Evolution of Language.* Cambridge: Harvard University Press.

Dunbar, Robin, Chris Knight, and Camilla Power. 1999. *The Evolution of Culture.* New Brunswick: Rutgers University Press.

Gamble, Clive. 1993. *Timewalkers: The Prehistory of Global Colonization.* Cambridge: Harvard University Press.

Jolly, Alison. 1999. *Lucy's Legacy: Sex and Intelligence in Human Evolution.* Cambridge: Harvard University Press.

Keeley, Lawrence H. 1996. *War before Civilization: The Myth of the Peaceful Savage.* New York: Oxford University Press.

Kingdon, Jonathan. 1993. *Self-Made Man: Human Evolution from Eden to Extinction.* New York: John Wiley & Sons.

Kossy, Donna. 2001. *Strange Creations: Aberrant Ideas of Human Origins from Ancient Astronauts to Aquatic Apes.* Los Angeles: Feral House.

Laland, Kevin N. and Gillian R. Brown. 2002. *Sense and Nonsense: Evolutionary Perspectives on Human Behavior.* New York: Oxford University Press.

Leakey, Richard. 1994. *The Origin of Humankind.* New York: Basic Books.

Lewin, Roger. 1993. *The Origin of Modern Humans.* New York: Basic Books.

Lieberman, P. 1991. *Uniquely Human: The Evolution of Speech, Thought, and Selfless Behavior.* Cambridge: Harvard University Press.

Lynch, Aaron. 1996. *Thought Contagion: How Belief Spreads Through Society.* New York: Basic Books.

Miller, Geoffrey. 2000. *The Mating Mind: How Sexual Choice Shaped the Evolution of Human Nature.* New York: Anchor Books.

Mithen, Steven. 1996. *The Prehistory of the Mind: The Cognition of Art, Religion, and Science.* London: Thames and Hudson.

Parker, Sue Taylor, and Michael L. McKinney. 1999. *Origin of Intelligence: The Evolution of Cognitive Development in Monkeys, Apes, and Humans.* Baltimore: The John Hopkins University Press.

Pinker, Steven. 1994. *The Language Instinct: How the Mind Creates Language.* New York: HarperCollins.

Plotkin, Henry. 1998. *Evolution in Mind: An Introduction to Evolutionary Psychology.* Cambridge: Harvard University Press.

Potts, Rick. 1996. *Human Descent: The Consequences of Ecological Instability.* New York: William Morrow.

Quiatt, Duane, and Junichiro Itani, eds. 1994. *Hominid Culture in Primate Perspective.* Boulder: University Press of Colorado.

Ridley, Matt. 1993. *The Red Queen: Sex and the Evolution of Human Nature.* New York: Macmillan.

Sagan, Carl, and Ann Druyan. 1992. *Shadows of Forgotten Ancestors: A Search For Who We Are.* New York: Random House.

Schick, Kathy D., and Nicholas Toth. 1994. *Making Silent Stones Speak: Human Evolution and the Dawn of Technology.* New York: Simon & Schuster.

Shreeve, James. 1995. *The Neanderthal Enigma: Solving the Mystery of Modern Human Origins.* New York: Avon Books.

Stanley, Steven M. 1996. *Children of the Ice Age: How a Global Catastrophe Allowed Humans to Evolve.* New York: Harmony Books.

Stringer, Christopher, and Clive Gamble. 1993. *In Search of the Neanderthals.* New York: Thames & Hudson.

Stringer, Christopher, and Robin McKie. 1996. *African Exodus: The Origin of Modern Humanity.* New York: Henry Holt.

Swisher, Carl C., III, Garniss H. Curtis, and Roger Lewin. 2000. *Java Man: How Two Geologists' Dramatic Discoveries Changed Our Understanding of the Evolutionary Path to Modern Humans.* New York: Scribner.

Tattersall, Ian. 1998. *Becoming Human: Evolution and Human Uniqueness.* San Diego: Harcourt Brace.

Tomasello, Michael. 1999. *The Cultural Origins of Human Cognition.* Cambridge: Harvard University Press.

Tudge, Colin. 1996. *The Time before History: Five Million Years of Human Impact.* New York: Scribner.

Waal, Frans B. M de. 2001. *Tree of Origin: What Primate Behavior Can Tell Us About Human Social Evolution.* Cambridge: Harvard University Press.

Walker, Alan, and Pat Shipman. 1996. *The Wisdom of Bones: In Search of Human Origins.* London: Weidenfeld and Nicolson.

Wilson, Edward O. 1978. *On Human Nature.* Cambridge: Harvard University Press.

Wright, Robert. 2000. *Nonzero: The Logic of Human Destiny.* New York: Pantheon Books.

Chapter 6

CIVILIZATIONS The chimpanzee who became ants

Armstrong, Karen. 1993. *A History of God: The 4000-year Quest of Judaism, Christianity, and Islam.* New York: Ballantine Books.

Atran, Scott. 2002. *In Gods We Trust: The Evolutionary Landscape of Religion.* Oxford: Oxford University Press.

Boyd, Robert and Peter Richerson. 2005. *The Origin and Evolution of Cultures.* Oxford: Oxford University Press.

Boyden, Stephen. 1987. *Western Civilization in Biological Perspective.* Oxford: Oxford University.

Boyer, Pascal. 2001. *Religion Explained: The Evolutionary Origins of Religious Thought.* New York: Basic Books.

Caras, Roger A. 1996. *A Perfect Harmony: The Intertwining Lives of Animals and Humans throughout History.* New York: Simon & Schuster.

Cohen, Mark N. 1989. *Health and the Rise of Civilization.* New Haven: Yale University.

Crosby, Alfred W., Jr. 1972. *The Colombian Exchange: Biological and Cultural Consequences of 1492*. New York: Cambridge University Press.

_______. 1986. *Ecological Imperialism: The Biological Expansion of Europe, 900-1900*. New York: Cambridge University Press.

_______. 1994. *Germs, Seeds, and Animals: Studies in Ecological History*. Armonk: M.E. Sharpe.

Diamond, Jared. 1997. *Guns, Germs, and Steel: The Fates of Human Societies*. New York: W. W. Norton.

Heiser, Charles B., Jr. 1990. *Seed to Civilization: The Story of Food.* Cambridge: Harvard University Press.

Johnson, Allen W., and Timothy Earle. 1987. *The Evolution of Human Societies: From Foraging Group to Agrarian State.* Stanford: Stanford University Press.

Lenski, Gerhard, Jean Lenski, and Patrick Nolan. 1991. *Human Societies: An Introduction to Macrosociology.* New York: McGraw-Hill.

Maryanski, Alexandra, and Jonathan H. Turner. 1992. *The Social Cage: Human Nature and the Evolution of Society.* Stanford: Stanford University Press.

McNeill, William H. 1992. *The Global Condition: Conquerors, Catastrophes, and Community*. Princeton: Princeton University Press.

Nikiforuk, Andrew. 1991. *The Fourth Horseman: A Short History of Epidemics, Plagues, Famines, and Other Scourges*. New York: M. Evans.

Ponting, Clive. 1991. *A Green History of the World*. New York: Penguin.

Schele, Linda, and David Freidel. 1990. *A Forest of Kings: The Untold Story of the Ancient Maya*. New York: William Morrow.

Serpell, James. 1986. *In the Company of Animals: A Study of Human-Animal Relationships*. New York: Basil Blackwell.

Stark, Rodney. 2003. *For the Glory of God: How Monotheism Led to Reformations, Science, Witch-Hunts, and the End of Slavery.* Princeton: Princeton University Press.

Toussaint-Samat, Maguelonne. 1992. *History of Food.* Cambridge: Blackwell.

Wilson, David Sloan. 2002. *Darwin's Cathedra: Evolution, Religion, and the Nature of Society.* Chicago: The University of Chicago Press.

Chapter 7

MACHINES The geese who laid the golden eggs

Adas, Michael. 1989. *Machines as the Measure of Men: Science, Technology, and Ideologies of Western Dominance.* Ithaca: Cornell University Press.

Basalla, George. 1988. *The Evolution of Technology.* New York: Cambridge University Press.

Buchanan, R. A. 1994. *The Power of the Machine: The Impact of Technology from 1700 to the Present.* New York: Penguin Books.

Burke, James, and Robert Ornstein. 1997. *The Axemaker's Gift: Technology's Capture and Control of Our Minds and Culture.* New York: G.P. Putnam's Sons.

Jones, Eric, Lionel Frost, and Colin White. 1993. *Coming Full Circle: An Economic History of the Pacific Rim.* Boulder: Westview.

Landes, David S. 1998. *The Wealth and Poverty of Nations: Why Some Are So Rich and Some Are So Poor.* New York: W. W. Norton.

Mazlish, Bruce. 1993. *The Fourth Discontinuity: The Co-evolution of Humans and Machines.* New Haven: Yale University Press.

McClellan, James E., III, and Harold Dorn. 1999. *Science and Technology in World History: An Introduction.* Baltimore: The John Hopkins University Press.

McNeill, William H. 1982. *The Pursuit of Power: Technology, Armed Force, and Society since A.D. 1000.* Chicago: University of Chicago Press.

Mokyr, Joel. 1990. *The Lever of Riches: Technological Creativity and Economic Progress.* Oxford: Oxford University Press.

Pacey, Arnold. 1992. *Technology in World Civilization.* Cambridge: MIT Press.

Rosenberg, Nathan, and L. E. Birdzell, Jr. 1986. *How the West Grew Rich: The Economic Transformation of the Industrial World.* New York: Basic Books.

Sass, Stephen L. 1998. *The Substance of Civilization: Materials and Human History from the Stone Age to the Age of Silicon.* New York: Arcade.

White, Lynn, Jr. 1962. *Medieval Technology and Social Change.* Oxford: Clarendon.

Chapter 8

SCIENTISTS The curious cats who pried open Pandora's box

Desmond, Adrian, and James Moore. 1991. *Darwin: The Life of a Tormented Evolutionist.* New York: W. W. Norton.

Dunbar, Robin. 1995. *The Trouble with Science.* Cambridge: Harvard University Press.

Ferguson, Kitty. 1999. *Measuring the Universe: Our Historic Quest to Chart the Horizons of Space and Time.* New York: Walker.

Gatti, Hilary. 1999. *Giordano Bruno and Renaissance Science.* Ithaca: Cornell University Press.

Gross, Paul R., and Norman Levitt. 1994. *Higher Superstition: The Academic Left and Its Quarrels with Science.* Baltimore: John Hopkins University.

Hirshfeld, Alan W. 2001. *Parallax: The Race to Measure the Cosmos.* New York: W.H. Freeman.

Horgan, John. 1996. *The End of Science: Facing the Limits of Knowledge in the Twilight of the Scientific Age.* Reading: Addison Press.

Huff, Toby E. 1993. *The Rise of Early Modern Science: Islam, China, and the West.* New York: Cambridge University Press.

Kuhn, Thomas S. 1957. *The Copernican Revolution: Planetary Astronomy in the Development of Western Thought.* Cambridge: Harvard University Press.

Levitt, Norman. 1999. *Prometheus Bedeviled: Science and the Contradictions of Contemporary Culture.* New Brunswick: Rutgers University Press.

Maddox, John. 1998. *What Remains to be Discovered: Mapping the Secrets of the Universe, the Origins of Life, and the Future of the Human Race.* New York: Simon & Schuster.

Mendoza, Ramon G. 1995. *The Acentric Labyrinth: Giordano Bruno's Prelude to Contemporary Cosmology.* Shaftesbury: Element Books.

Midgley, Mary. 1992. *Science as Salvation: A Modern Myth and Its Meaning.* London: Routledge.

Newton-Smith, W. H. 1981. *The Rationality of Science.* Boston: Routledge & Kegan-Paul.

Rescher, Nicholas. 1999. *The Limits of Science.* Pittsburgh: University of Pittsburgh Press.

Rhodes, Richard. 1995. *Dark Sun: The Making of the Hydrogen Bomb.* New York: Simon & Schuster.

Shattuck, Roger. 1996. *Forbidden Knowledge: From Prometheus to Pornography.* New York: St. Martin's.

Silver, Brian L. 1998. *The Ascent of Science.* New York: Oxford University Press.

Sobel, David, and William J. H. Andrews. 1998. *The Illustrated Longitude: The True Story of a Lone Genius Who Solved the Greatest Scientific Problem of His Time.* New York: Walker.

Stevenson, Leslie, and Henry Byerly. 1995. *The Many Faces of Science.* Boulder: Westview.

White, Michael. 2001. *Acid Tongues and Tranquil Dreamers: Tales of Bitter Rivalry That Fueled the Advancement of Science and Technology.* New York: William Morrow.

_______. 2002. *The Pope and the Heretic: The True Story of Giordano Bruno, The Man Who Dared to Defy the Roman Inquisition.* New York: William Morrow.

Wolpert, Lewis. 1992. *The Unnatural Nature of Science.* Cambridge: Harvard University Press.

Ziman, John. 2000. *Real Science: What It Is, And What It Means.* Cambridge: Cambridge University Press.

Chapter 9

CHIMPANZEE PARADISE High-tech Garden of Eden

Maser, Chris. 1992. *Global Imperative: Harmonizing Culture & Nature.* Walpole: Stillpoint.

Nesse, Randolph M., and George C. Williams. 1994. *Why We Get Sick: The New Science of Darwinian Medicine.* New York: Times Books.

Stent, Gunther S. 1969. *The Coming of the Golden Age.* Garden City: Natural History Press.

Wilson, Edward O. 2003. *The Future of Life.* New York: Alfred A. Knopf.

Chapter 10

BOOM & BUST May the punishment fit the crime

Alley, Richard B. 2000. *The Two-Mile Time Machine: Ice Cores, Abrupt Climate Change, and Our Future.* Princeton: Princeton University Press.

Eldredge, Niles. 1995. *Dominion: Can Nature and Culture Co-Exist?* New York: Henry Holt.

Garrett, Laurie. 1994. *The Coming Plague: Newly Emerging Diseases in a World Out of Balance.* New York: Farrar, Straus, and Giroux.

Greider, William. 1997. *One World, Ready or Not: The Manic Logic of Global Capitalism.* New York: Simon and Schuster.

Kolata, Gina. 1999. *The Story of the Great Influenza Pandemic of 1918 and the Search for the Virus That Caused It.* New York: Farrar, Straus and Giroux.

Leakey, Richard, and Roger Lewin. 1995. *The Sixth Extinction: Patterns of Life and the Future of Humankind.* New York: Doubleday.

Leslie, John. 1996. *The End of the World: The Science and Ethics of Human Extinction.* London: Routledge.

Palast, Greg. 2003. *The Best Democracy Money Can Buy: The Truth About Corporate Cons, Globalization, and High-Finance Fraudsters.* New York: Plume Books.

Preston, Richard. 1994. *The Hot Zone.* New York: Random House.

Ryan, Frank. 1992. *The Forgotten Plague: How the Battle Against Tuberculosis Was Won—and Lost.* Boston: Back Bay Books.

Schneider, Stephen H. 1997. *Laboratory Earth: The Planetary Gamble We Can't Afford to Lose.* New York: Basic Books.

Tainter, Joseph A. 1988. *The Collapse of Complex Societies.* New York: Cambridge University Press.

Tudge, Colin. 1992. *Last Animals at the Zoo: How Mass Extinction Can Be Stopped.* Washington: Island Press.

Ward, Peter D., and Donald Brownlee. 2002. *The Life and Death of Planet Earth: How the New Science of Astrobiology Charts the Ultimate Fate of Our World.* New York: Henry Holt.

Chapter 11

PLANETARY SUPERORGANISM All together on the global farm

Bailey, Ronald. 2002. *Global Warming and Other Eco-Myths: How the Environmental Movement Uses False Science to Scare Us to Death.* New York: Prima.

Botkin, Daniel B. 1990. *Discordant Harmonies: A New Ecology for the Twenty-First Century.* Oxford: Oxford University.

Brown, Lester R. 2001. *Eco-Economy: Building an Economy for the Earth.* New York: W. W. Norton.

Coon, Carleton S. 2000. *Cultural Wars and the Global Village.* New York: Prometheus Books.

Hawken, Paul, Amory Lovins, and L. Hunter Lovins. 1999. *Natural Capitalism.* Boston: Back Bay Books.

Heilbroner, Robert. 1995. *Visions of the Future.* Oxford: Oxford University.

Kaufman, Wallace. 1994. *No Turning Back: Dismantling the Fantasies of Environmental Thinking.* New York: Basic Books.

Kennedy, Paul. 1993. *Preparing for the Twenty-First Century.* New York: Vintage Books.

Korten, David C. 1999. *The Post-Corporate World: Life after Capitalism.* San Francisco: Berrett-Koehler.

Lewis, Martin W. 1992. *Green Delusions: An Environmentalist Critique of Radical Environmentalism.* Durham: Duke University.

Laszlo, Ervin. 2001. *Macroshift: Navigating the Transformation to a Sustainable World.* San Francisco: Berrett-Koehler Publishers.

Ray, Paul H., and Sherry Ruth Anderson. 2000. *The Cultural Creatives: How 50 Million People are Changing the World.* New York: Three Rivers Press.

Simon, Julian L. 1981. *The Ultimate Resource.* Princeton: Princeton University Press.

Chapter 12

STAR TREK Our descendants inherit the galaxy

Broderick, Damien. 2001. *The Spike: How Our Lives Are Being Transformed by Rapidly Advancing Technologies.* New York: Tom Doherty Associates.

Coren, Richard. 1998. *The Evolutionary Trajectory: The Growth of Information in the History and Future of Earth.* Amsterdam: Gordon and Breach.

Drexter, K. Eric. 1986. *Engines of Creation: The Coming Era of Nanotechnology.* New York: Anchor Press.

Drexter, K. Eric, Chris Peterson, and Gayle Pergamit. 1993. *Unbounding the Future: The Nanotechnology Revolution.* New York: Quill William Morrow.

Dyson, George. 1997. *Darwin among the Machines: The Evolution of Global Intelligence.* Reading: Perseus Books.

Finney, Ben R., and Eric M. Jones. 1985. *Interstellar Migration and the Human Experience.* Berkley: University of California Press.

Goonatilake, Susantha. 1999. *Merged Evolution: Long–Term Implications of Biotechnology and Information Technology.* Amsterdam: Gordon and Breach.

Guthke, Karl S. 1990. *The Last Frontier: Imagining Other Worlds from the Copernican Revolution to Modern Science Fiction.* Ithaca: Cornell University Press.

Kurzwell, Ray. 1999. *The Age of Spiritual Machines: When Computers Exceed Human Intelligence.* New York: Viking.

Levy, Steven. 1992. *Artificial Life: The Quest for a New Creation.* New York: Pantheon Books.

Moravec, Hans. 1988. *Mind Children: The Future of Robot and Human Intelligence.* Cambridge: Harvard University Press.

_______. 1999. *Robot: Mere Machine to Transcendent Mind.* New York: Oxford University Press.

Stock, Gregory. 2002. *Redesigning Humans: Our Inevitable Genetic Future.* Boston: Houghton Mifflin.

Worster, Donald. 1994. *Nature's Economy: A History of Ecological Ideas* 2nd ed. New York: Cambridge University Press.

Index

C

D

E

F

G

H

I

J

K

L

M

Q

R

S

T

U

V

W

Y

Z